CHRISTIAN UNIVERSALISM

God's Good News For All People

Eric Stetson

Sparkling Bay Books

Christian Universalism: God's Good News For All People

Published by:
Sparkling Bay Books

ISBN: 0-9670631-8-3

Eric Stetson has been a spiritual seeker his whole life. After exploring various religions and philosophies, he became a Christian in 2002 and began attending an evangelical church. But he struggled with the doctrine of eternal hell – how could a loving God punish some souls forever, just because they didn't measure up to His lofty standards in one mortal life? This book is the result of several years of study of this crucial question. Stetson's careful examination of the Bible in its original languages and the teachings of early church fathers and saints led him to conclude that hell is not an eternal torment, but a reformative process that souls must go through so that all can eventually be redeemed and reconciled with their Creator.

TABLE OF CONTENTS

But the angel said to them,
"Do not be afraid. I bring you good news of great joy that will be for all the people. Today in the town of David a Savior has been born to you; He is Christ the Lord."

Luke 2:10-11

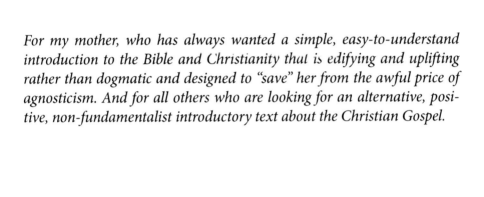

For my mother, who has always wanted a simple, easy-to-understand introduction to the Bible and Christianity that is edifying and uplifting rather than dogmatic and designed to "save" her from the awful price of agnosticism. And for all others who are looking for an alternative, positive, non-fundamentalist introductory text about the Christian Gospel.

A Note On Bible Verses:

All quotations from the Bible in this book are from the New International Version (NIV), unless otherwise noted. The NIV is a very popular, easy-to-read translation. However, in some cases this Bible version mistranslates verses that conflict with evangelical Christian doctrines. The New Revised Standard Version, especially the HarperCollins Study Bible, is recommended for those who want a somewhat more neutral and academic view of the scriptures. Bible verses in this book that are taken from this translation are noted as NRSV.

Unfortunately, no version of the Bible is completely free from distortions of the original Greek and Hebrew text, so readers are encouraged to consult a variety of Bible translations and study the meaning of words in the original languages when confusion or controversy may arise. The Young's Literal Translation and Rotherham Literal Translation are particularly useful in cases where word-for-word accuracy is essential. Strong's Exhaustive Concordance of the Bible can also be a helpful guide—though it has its own biases and inaccuracies on certain key words.

Out of respect for the Deity, and for the sake of clarity and stylistic consistency, pronouns referring to God are always capitalized in this book, even though the Bible versions used do not originally capitalize them.

Introduction

A Story of Christian Faith

Max Christian was a Christian man—a *very* Christian man. He went to church regularly, attended a Bible study group, and always voted for the candidate that talked the most about faith and family values. His church was the kind where a homosexual, an unmarried couple, or a girl baring her pierced navel would feel distinctly unwelcome. Max had a bumper sticker on his truck that said "In case of Rapture, this vehicle will be unoccupied."

Perhaps the reason why Max was so religious was that he was well acquainted with sin and the need for God's forgiveness. Every Friday night after work, Max would go out drinking, gambling, and visiting strip clubs with his buddies. When he got home in the middle of the night, he would threaten or hit his wife if she didn't do exactly what he wanted. Sometimes, after a particularly bad time at the poker table and a few too many beers, he would be so filled with anger that he would end up chasing his son around the house swinging a belt with a big studded buckle, cursing and putting the fear of God into the boy.

Come Sunday morning, Max Christian would always be starched and ready for church, with his submissive wife and son in tow, and he would hold his hands high in the air during the service as the congregation sang about "the blood of Jeee-sus." He would say, "Yes Lord, heavenly Father, wash away my sins in the blood of the Lamb!"—visibly trembling and begging for mercy. He felt sorry for his sins and believed the right doctrines, and he knew that was all that mattered. Emerging from this weekly religious experience, he always felt like a new man, born again in Christ and blessed with a grace that no Hindu or athe-

9

ist could ever enjoy. It was as if his sins never happened—at least until next Friday night, when the whole cycle would start all over again.

Max's son was a sensitive lad who thought deeply about the world around him and the meaning of life. When his grandmother died, he struggled with the fact that she had never professed faith in Christ and did not attend church, even though she was a very nice person and was the only one in his family that he felt really loved him. Her death left him worrying about whether she went to heaven or hell. Max, meanwhile, became even more zealous in his religious beliefs, reminding his son that "you don't want to end up in hell like your grandmother who wasn't a Christian," every time he disobeyed or questioned anything. When he finally told his father he didn't want to go to church anymore because he didn't agree with some of their beliefs, Max erupted in rage and beat his son until he pleaded for mercy.

It didn't help matters that Max's son was interested in art and theater, not football and hunting. He had no real friends in the conservative town where they lived, his grades were slipping, and soon in his despair he turned to drugs and pornography. He was terrified that his father would find out about his addictions. Unable to deal with the stress of these issues, he took the family gun one lonely night and shot himself in the head. After that, Max's wife also began to question her faith—and her blind obedience to her ultra-religious husband.

One day they got into a huge argument. Outdoors, the sky turned black as a tornado was approaching, while inside, angry words flew, along with small objects. Right before the storm tore apart their house, Max Christian's wife shouted to her husband, "Your religion, your Bible, your church and your God have destroyed our family! I don't want anything more to do with you and your God—ever!" Max was down on his knees praying to God, repenting of his latest round of sins and pledging renewed allegiance to the cross of Christ, asking for the blood of Jesus to cleanse him and make his soul white as snow. And then both Max and his wife were lifted up by the twister and died.

Max suddenly found himself in a great throne room, filled with gold and precious jewels. God was sitting on the throne. Jesus came and said, "Here is Max Christian, and though his sins were many, his faith has saved him. Because of the atoning power of my righteous sacrifice on the cross, all his sins are forgiven and he is justified and glorified." Angels began singing, and Max was ushered into heaven.

"What happened to the rest of my family?" he asked. Jesus pointed down, and Max Christian saw his unbelieving wife and son writhing and screaming in pain, burning in a lake of liquid fire. He also saw his son's grandmother there. They were there along with teeming masses of souls—billions and billions—many of them dark-skinned people who worshipped pagan gods and idols and never even heard the Gospel of Jesus Christ. "Alas," said Jesus. "They did not have the right religious beliefs to qualify for heaven, so they must spend eternity in hell."

Max felt a twinge of sadness. "That's a shame," he said somberly. Fortunately, it was just a fleeting moment of pity. Soon enough, he forgot about the never-ending agonies of the damned and was happy again, ready to enjoy an eternity of paradise with his Lord. "Bibles here for everyone!" cried an angel in a voice like the sound of a trumpet. "King James Version only, of course." *Of course!* Max thought to himself. *I knew I had it right all along.*

The Bad News Gospel

Do you see something wrong with this picture? Sure, this is just a caricature, but it is surprisingly similar to what many Christians actually believe about the way things work in our universe. If they don't believe in this evangelical Protestant version of reality, then they might believe in a Catholic version, in which somebody like "Max Christian" will get to heaven by consistently attending mass, scrupulously confessing to the priest and taking all the sacraments of the Roman Church—while heretics and pagans will be eternally condemned for their mortal sins and non-belief.

Every day, all over the world, people are sharing the Gospel of Jesus Christ. The word "gospel" means *good news*. But is the gospel being preached from pulpits, spread by missionaries in foreign lands, and believed by millions of souls in Christian churches and denominations really the Good News that was taught by Jesus Christ and his apostles 2000 years ago? No, it is not. The Christian religion has lost its way, exchanging the hopeful message of Jesus, Paul, Peter, John, and their earliest disciples for a different doctrine invented by church theologians, imposed by Roman emperors, and established as the central teaching of "orthodox Christianity" centuries ago. It has been so long since this change occurred that most people have no idea what happened, what the faith of Christ once was—and what it is supposed to be. Only through open-minded study and reflection can people break free of the false version of Christianity that masquerades as truth.

This book is a brief layman's introduction to the Christian Gospel from a universalist perspective. Whether you're a Christian or a non-Christian, you will find a very different view of Christianity in this book than what is normally presented as the Gospel. The alternative message of Christian Universalism is Biblically sound and easy to understand. If you're looking for a fresh perspective on basic Christian teachings, this book will radically change the way you see the Gospel. The next time someone shoves a tract called "The Burning Hell" in your face and asks whether you're saved, you will know why they believe what they do—and why they *shouldn't*, if they want to be a true Christian.

But how could that be? Christianity says to the world, "repent or be damned… forever." Isn't that what Jesus taught, and what the Bible makes explicitly clear: that non-believers and sinners will go to hell, a place of eternal torment and separation from God, with no hope of ever gaining release? Those who repent of their sins and accept Jesus as Lord will be forgiven and blessed with eternal life in heaven, whereas those who remain in their sins and without faith in Christ will be doomed to everlasting fire. Boiled down to its basic essence, this is what the Christian Gospel is all about, right?

Sadly, this is what passes for Christianity in many people's minds. It is hardly good news—but this is what is most often shared as the "Gospel." Instead of remaining blissfully ignorant of God's ways, we are informed of the bad news that the majority of people who have ever lived are condemned to a permanent state of pain, never to be reconciled with their Creator. A small minority—those lucky enough to be born in the right place and time to hear about Christ, and intelligent enough to understand and accept him—will be spared from damnation and receive salvation. But only if they believe in the correct version of Christianity, join the right church or denomination, have a "born again" experience, and obey certain moral laws so as to avoid losing their salvation to the power of sin. It all depends on who you ask and which building you are worshipping in. One is never free from the lingering fear that hell could await after death, that one might not believe or act correctly enough to escape the horrific fires of doom where the majority of human beings will suffer forever.

That is supposed to be good news? If that's what Christianity is all about, no wonder so many people today are deciding that it's a hypocritical and disgusting religion. Preachers talk about God's love, His forgiveness and mercy. But they remind us—though in most churches not usually so bluntly, to avoid offending our innate sensibilities—that *the very same God* is also a God of unquenchable wrath, vengeance, and cruelty. And then they have the nerve to ask us to develop a personal relationship with such a God. How about a personal relationship with Hitler? I'm sure he could be nice to his family and friends, too. But get on his wrong side, and watch out!—you're headed for the ovens. Is God not much different than an evil dictator, except in his ability to keep the fires burning and to keep ruling over a trembling humanity forever?

Fundamentalism vs. Universalism

Christian Fundamentalists would like everyone to believe in their version of Christianity as if it were the only way of understanding the Gospel. In reality, they present the world with a false gospel that turns many people away from God entirely and leaves many of those who convert to their religion in a state of spiritual immaturity, never able to get beyond the animalistic fear of punishment in the afterlife. The fundamentalists envision God as a tyrant who has so little love and mercy for the people he created that He would fry billions of them forever in a cosmic torture chamber—just because they accidentally chose the wrong religious beliefs or failed to repent of some sins before they die. They erroneously claim that this is what Jesus Christ taught—and they get away with it because many people simply don't know any better. Even the words of the Bible have been twisted and mistranslated to support an incorrect view. No wonder most people don't realize the fundamentalist convert-or-burn version is not the true message of the Gospel.

Christian Universalism is the view that the original Biblical Gospel of Jesus Christ—as taught by Jesus himself and the apostles, and as foreshadowed by the prophets of the Old Testament—is a message of hope for all people, the promise of God's saving grace made available to all mankind and never to be withdrawn. It is a vision of a God who is both just *and* merciful, who in His very nature *is* love, and who is always in the business of saving, reconciling, and transforming souls regardless of what they believed or how many sins they committed during one mortal life. Christian Universalists, in contrast to fundamentalists, believe that Christianity is about the boundless goodness of God and His divine plan for *all* people. God will not settle for a forever divided universe, where some souls are reunited with their Creator in heaven and others eternally separated in the misery of hell. No, the real God is infinitely more powerful and benevolent than that. God wants all to be saved, and He has the power to accomplish it in the fullness of time.

The truth is, *fundamental* Christianity has little to do with the "fundamentalist" message preached by so many in Jesus' name. The fundamentals of Christian faith include some things taught by believers in traditional Christian orthodoxy, to be sure, but not the whole package. The central teaching of Christian Fundamentalism—that many, probably the vast majority of souls ever created must go to hell for eternity because they failed to accept Jesus Christ as their Lord and Savior, and that God cannot or will not resolve this problem—is a seductive and repulsive falsehood cleverly disguised as the gospel truth. It is seductive to those who want heaven to be an exclusive club reserved only for people who believe like them; and it is repulsive to people who expect a more sublime and glorious outcome of God's plan rather than something that could only be invented by the fallen human ego.

Finding the True Path of Christ

Millions of people today are coming to the belief in universal salvation. Many of them are sincere, Bible-believing Christians. They attend churches of various denominations and come from diverse backgrounds. Each one has a unique story to tell of how God led them— sometimes gently, sometimes dramatically—to move beyond their former belief in eternal hell and rigid church doctrines and to embrace an inclusive view of salvation and an optimistic view of God and His plan for our lives and our universe. My own story is told in this book, and this introduction to Christian Universalism is the fruit of my desire to share what I have learned about the Gospel with others. The reason I wrote it is so that many more people will have their own stories to share—discovering a different kind of Christianity and being transformed from the inside out by the knowledge of God's unconditional and all-consuming love.

This might be your first time learning of any kind of Christian Gospel other than the harsh message of fundamentalists, who have told you you're going to hell unless you belong to their church, or unless you pray a certain way or believe certain religious teachings—who have told you your loved ones who died without professing faith in Christ are lost forever. You may have followed this religious system out of fear of doing otherwise or because you were raised to believe it. Or you may have rejected it in disgust and thrown God out of your life along with the nasty fundamentalist Christian creed. I invite you to consider the alternative, the *Good News* Gospel of Christian Universalism that is the original message of the Christian faith. It is a message that our hurting world desperately needs to hear today. It is a message that can truly *change* souls rather than just "winning" them.

In this book, we will examine the Biblical alternative to Christian Fundamentalism: the positive and uplifting view of Christianity called Christian Universalism. We will discover that the Bible, when properly translated and interpreted, supports the optimistic view of salvation called universal or ultimate reconciliation, rather than the more popular ideas of eternal damnation or annihilation of the wicked. We will discuss some of the objections people commonly raise to Christian Universalism and answer them. We will explore some of the more profound implications of the universalist interpretation of Christianity for the nature of God, the meaning of the life, death, and resurrection of Christ, and human nature and destiny. We will survey the history of Christian thought concerning salvation and the fate of those who do not follow Christ in their life on earth, and we will see how the rise of the doctrine of eternal torment led to terrible consequences both in society as a whole and in the lives of individual Christians. We will discuss the rebirth of universalist theology in modern times, and we will consider the importance of the Good News of Christian Universalism in today's world, with the frightening rise of religious fundamentalism—both fundamentalist Christianity and other extremist forms of faith—that is the source of increasing levels of division, hatred, and even violence in the name of God.

I hope that readers will see the faith of Christ in a whole new light—the light of truth as revealed in the Bible and in the human heart and mind, free from the darkness that has been spread by ignorant fundamentalism throughout history and in the present day. Christianity is seen in the popular culture as a religion that offers salvation only for believers and the torments of a never-ending hell for everyone else. That must change. Only the universalist form of Christianity can move people to love God with a true love freely given, and to serve God and their fellow man with a depth of compassion that springs only from the knowledge that all people are God's children and all will meet again one day in our Father's house.

So let's turn off the fiery televangelists and throw out the angry tracts that say "confess Christ or else…" and find a real reason to believe in him and walk in the way he showed us so many centuries ago. It is a path that is often forgotten, but which is ever relevant and leads to an outcome infinitely greater than anything that is usually preached from the pulpit. It is a path that leads out of hell and into heaven—a path that all souls someday shall tread. The first step is to discover who God really is, who we really are, and how we have been deceived into thinking the divine path is something very different from what it really is. Trusting in the Spirit to lead us to the truth, let's begin the journey!

What the Bible Really Teaches about Sin, Judgment and Salvation

The Bible, including both the Old and New Testaments, is the foundational text of Christianity. Christians of all types turn to this great text for inspiration and revelation of spiritual truth. Therefore, if we seek to learn the message of the Christian faith, it is important that we examine what the Bible really teaches about important issues. Perhaps the most important of all is the relationship between man and God, and how this relationship can be disturbed and restored. That, in a nutshell, is what the Bible is all about.

What Is the Bible?

Over the course of several centuries, many authors wrote the books that have been compiled into the official collection, or *canon*, we know today as "The Holy Bible." A few books have been included or excluded from the canon by different branches of Christianity, meaning that the Roman Catholic, Eastern Orthodox, and Protestant versions of the Bible are not entirely the same. Each author who contributed to the Bible had his own perspective, ideas, and opinions, shaped by the influences of social status, culture, and prevailing beliefs of the time. If all these people were gathered together in one room, there would be some heated debates about religious issues! Nevertheless, the work of a greater Author is evident in their writings, especially when viewed together as one. That is why the Bible has survived to inspire generation after generation of human beings, and is the world's most popular book.

Before we begin to look at the Bible's teachings, let me be clear about how I view the scriptures. I am not a believer in the fundamentalist doctrine called *Biblical inerrancy*. Belief in Biblical inerrancy leads to intellectual contortions, as sincere believers try to fit every Bible verse into some kind of perfect doctrinal framework, which cannot be maintained except by rationalization and explaining away problematic passages and contradictions. Authoritarianism and heavy-handed suppression of free thought are an all-too-common result.

There's a saying that *the devil* is the greatest Bible scholar. Indeed, the adversary often puts it into the hearts of Christians to use the Bible as ammunition to fiercely argue the finer points of doctrine, thus missing the larger point of the holy scriptures. Spraying forth a whole lot of Bible verses like bullets from a machine gun is not my style, and I don't think it's very useful for people who strive to think in a broad-minded and comprehensive way, which in my opinion is more likely to lead to true understanding. That's why I don't claim that we can figure out exactly what to believe on every issue through Bible study. There is a place for the guidance of the Holy Spirit, for reason, and various other ways of discovering truth.

What I *do* claim—and will seek to show in Part One—is that the Bible is a book of great spiritual wisdom, containing much revelation of God's nature and will and relationship with human beings; and that if we look at the Bible as a whole, we will find certain important themes running through it that are positive and uplifting, revealing a God whose love and forgiveness are greater than His anger and wrath. We need not believe in an inerrant Bible to believe in a Bible that is authoritative and relevant to our lives, which in its most central messages speaks with one voice—a voice of a God who cares more deeply about the wellbeing of each individual He has created than we could ever imagine, and who has the power to bring all His wonderful plans to fruition.

Basic Biblical Concepts

Anyone who has been exposed to Christianity knows something about the concepts of sin, judgment, and salvation. These are classic, essential Christian ideas about the relationship between man and his Creator. But lost in the popular view of these concepts is the simple truth of what they signify in Biblical terms, stripped of the accumulated images religious leaders have created over centuries of "spinning" the faith for the masses.

The Bible is a story of man's fall into sin, divine judgment as a consequence, and the hope of salvation to overcome sin and bring God's judgments to an end. *Sin* is not some morbid, guilt-ridden thing that should cause us to turn away from Christian teaching. No, in fact sin is the very act of turning away from God. That is what sin means: to go in the wrong direction, to *miss the mark*. When Christians say that "all people are sinners," what this means is simply that nobody is perfect. We all have a tendency to sometimes fail to do what we should do, or to do things we shouldn't do, or to take the wrong path or make a mistake. That is the reality of sin—and it is a central focus of the Bible.

Why should the Bible be so focused on the fact that humans are imperfect and miss the mark? Well, because God wants to perfect us. God does not reveal our sinfulness to us so that we can sulk in our guilt, but so that we can change our ways and become better human beings! God's *judgment* is how that excellent goal is accomplished. When people sin, God is liable to judge them as a natural *consequence* of their sin, in order to make them see the error of their ways and thus "save" them from the mistake they made. When divine judgment occurs, it can be pretty unpleasant and may feel like harsh punishment. But the point of it is to *correct* us. This is a basic teaching of the Bible which we will be discussing throughout this book.

How does God save us through judgment? *Salvation,* the process of being saved from sin and made more perfect in God's sight, has several steps from start to finish. First, there must come *repentance* on the part of the sinner. To repent simply means to *change one's mind*, to acknowledge one's mistake. It is not about wallowing in guilt, though a feeling of guilt might be an initial part of it. When we repent of our sin, we are making a positive, purposeful acknowledgement that we have thought or done wrong, and that we are actively seeking to change our ways, so as to walk in the direction of God rather than away from Him and His ways. The experience of divine judgment—the suffering, the loss and pain, whether physical, mental, or spiritual—is what enables us to come to a point of repentance. Judgment is therefore a beneficial gift from God for our wellbeing, because it starts us on the path of salvation.

After repentance comes *atonement*. Atonement means *making amends*. The sinner who has repented must make amends to the one who was sinned against, either another person who is the victim of one's sin, or God Himself who hurts whenever His earthly children turn away from Him and against His way. Atoning to God could be accomplished through newfound faith in God's willingness to forgive, or through some form of penance to make up for past wrongdoing. If one cannot fully atone for one's own sins, another could make a vicarious atonement on one's behalf to help settle the accounts of good and evil. However it might occur, justice is affirmed and the negative effects of sin are balanced through the positive, compensating effects of atonement. There are different theories about this put forward in different parts of the Bible, but in general, the Bible affirms that atonement of some kind is a necessary part of salvation. We will come back to this topic when we discuss the atoning power of the cross of Christ in Part Two.

Forgiveness occurs when atonement is made for sin. The offended party *moves beyond the sin*, as if it never happened. Debts are canceled, trespasses are forgotten, and the sinner is no longer viewed as being in a state of transgression. In contrast to repentance, which is undertaken by the will of the sinner, forgiveness is the step that must be taken by the one sinned against. Although there may be a will to forgive no matter what, full and total forgiveness is not manifested until repentance and atonement have occurred. This is the natural progression of the salvation process.

Finally, when the sinner is completely forgiven, there can be *reconciliation*. This is the condition of *returning to oneness* and friendly relations between beings, the one who sinned and the one sinned against—and it may be between human beings or between man and God. Reconciliation implies *restoration*, the renewal of the positive state of affairs before the sin occurred. In some sense, reconciliation also goes beyond merely restoring the sin-free condition, but actually deepens our relationship with the victim of our sin and with God, because we have passed through a difficult episode of imbalance and misdirection and have emerged on the other side at a higher level that would not have been possible otherwise. The sinner gains the maturity of greater understanding and moves closer to perfection through judgment and the salvation process.

What I have just described is the overall message of the Bible, without reference to any of the text's specific contents. Sin, judgment, and the salvation process of repentance, atonement, forgiveness and reconciliation are what constitute the central theme of the Judeo-Christian scriptures. This theme is to be found played out in individual Biblical stories as well as the book taken as a whole. In summary, the message of the Bible is that humans are imperfect, but there is a way that we can be perfected by a combination of God's actions and our own response.

Foreshadowing of Universal Reconciliation in the Old Testament

People often remark that the Old Testament presents God in a much harsher light than the New Testament. In the Hebrew scriptures, God is a deity of fiery wrath who inflicts vengeance upon His wayward people, often in brutal ways. The laws of Moses are strict, and punishments are harsh. God is jealous, angry, and obsessed with righteousness and holiness—and mere humans who don't live up to His standards are like ants to be crushed under His mighty foot. So goes the common perception. Surely, if significant evidence of an eternal hell is to be found in the Bible, it would be in this harsher part of the scriptures, right?

Would it surprise you to learn that there is no evidence of the teaching of eternal hell in the Old Testament *at all*? That's right, the Hebrew scriptures do not contain the idea of a place of never-ending torment beyond the grave for the wicked. According to the Old Testament, when you die you go to *Sheol*—a dark, nondescript abode of the dead—regardless of how bad your sins were during your mortal life. There's no heavenly paradise or fiery torture chamber for the dead described in the holy books of ancient Judaism. The judgments of God were understood to come in this life, here on earth. Evil people would be punished during their lifetime, and good people would be rewarded. Or so it was in the view of early Jewish religious thinkers represented in the Bible. A few questioned this view, which would ultimately lead to further theological developments such as the teaching of the resurrection of the dead, which is more fully developed in the New Testament.

Many Christians are unaware that eternal hell is not a commonly held doctrine in Judaism. The Jewish religion evolved in a very different direction from Christianity on the issue of divine judgment. The overwhelming majority of post-Biblical rabbinic thought through the centuries has maintained a purgatorial view of hell, in which sinners must remain there only for a period of time until they have received a just penalty. This is because the Old Testament does not contain any references or warnings about sinners condemned to endure everlasting punishments in the afterlife, and it does contain much internal evidence that punishment for sin is always limited. To the degree that Jews believe in hell at all, it is generally not in the sense of eternal conscious torment. Christians have read this idea into the Jewish Bible based on their own faulty interpretations of the New Testament, which we will discuss later.

The Old Testament was more concerned with the fate of the Jewish people as a whole rather than the afterlife of individuals. And in general, the Old Testament is interested in judgment and salvation in a corporate sense, for tribes and nations, rather than each individual person. In the Hebrew scriptures we read about how God chose the people of Israel for special attention, gave them detailed moral standards to live by (the Law), and imposed judgments upon them collectively when their nation sinned against the Law.

One thing is clear: God never gives up on His people. No matter how much the Jews sinned against Him—and boy, did they sin a lot, according to the Bible—God never let judgment be the final doom of Israel. After judgment would *always* come salvation. God would always forgive sins and there was *no time limit* on God's forgiveness. God frequently sent prophets to warn Israel to turn from sin and repent, and often He patiently delayed imposing judgment until the sinfulness became intolerable. Then, if Israel still had failed to repent by some point in time, God would bring a limited judgment upon the nation to spur the people to repentance, but would not wipe out the entire Hebrew people leaving no Jews remaining. Instead, He made a covenant with Israel that they would always be His people and He would always be their God. Though the masses of the nation might be destroyed in war or exile or whatever other form of divine judgment that occurred, a remnant of Israel would always remain, and through this remnant would come repentance and salvation for Israel as a whole.

Even before God chose the Jews, the theme of salvation always following judgment is to be found in the Bible. For example, when "The LORD saw how great man's wickedness on the earth had become, and that every inclination of the thoughts of his heart was only evil all the time" (Gen. 6:5), God restrained Himself from totally destroying the people of the world. He preserved what was good among them—Noah and his family—and destroyed all the evil according to the story of the Flood. Then He restored humanity again by multiplying the descendents of Noah.

When the cities of Sodom and Gomorrah became thoroughly evil and depraved, God led out the one righteous man, Lot, from among them and destroyed the wicked who remained in a fiery judgment. Later on in the Old Testament, we read the amazing prophecy that God will "restore the fortunes of Sodom" (Ezek. 16:53)—amazing because this city was the archetypal symbol of extreme wickedness in the mind of the Jews, and was supposed to be "a wasteland forever" (Zeph. 2:9). God's plans always include keeping whatever is good with an ultimate goal of restoration after judgment upon evil.

The concept of a "righteous remnant" that would never be destroyed by God in His judgments is key to understanding the message of universal reconciliation, the belief that all will be saved in the end rather than being consigned to eternal torment or annihilation. Could it be that God would never completely destroy any individual human being or leave anyone in a permanent state of judgment and punishment—in the same way that God would never completely and permanently destroy humanity as a whole, or the corrupt cities of Sodom and Gomorrah, or Israel His chosen nation? Certainly that would be in keeping with the revealed character of God in the Bible. "You do not stay angry forever but delight to show mercy," says the prophet Micah about God (Mic. 7:18). "For His anger lasts only a moment..." we read in the Psalms (Ps. 30:5). "Give thanks to the LORD, for He is good; His love endures forever." (Ps. 106:1).[1] He is "the compassionate and gracious God" (Ex. 34:6), "slow to anger, abounding in love and forgiving sin and rebellion…" (Num. 14:18).[2]

God is in the business of destroying evil and saving what is good. Surely in the same way that there was a remnant of goodness in Noah's time and in Sodom and in the nation of Israel, there must be at least some tiny bit of goodness in each individual human being, even the most evil among us. If the presence of some good within an entity prevents God from destroying the entire thing because of the bad, then why would God refuse to save any individual, no matter how sinful? Nobody is 100% bad, totally irredeemable. God is in the salvation business, and He has the power to get the job done. His judgments have a purpose, and that purpose is not total and utter ruin. The "harsh" Old Testament teaches us this optimistic lesson.

God's Relationship with the Jews and All Humanity

The Bible is largely a book about the history—both political and religious—of the Jewish people. But that doesn't necessarily mean that God only cares about the Jews, or that His character should be different in how He relates to Gentiles. The New Testament emphasizes the idea that God treats the Jews and the Gentiles equally. As the Apostle Paul wrote, "There is neither Jew nor Greek, slave nor free, male nor female, for you are all one in Christ Jesus." (Gal. 3:28). Nevertheless, Paul himself was a Jew, as was Jesus and all the twelve apostles. Nearly the entire Bible, if not all of it, is believed to have been written by Jews. The difference is that the Jews who wrote the New Testament believed that God was expanding His covenant relationship with the Jews to include all people through the Gospel of Jesus Christ.

Therefore, in light of the fact that the story of God's relationship with man as told in the Bible is a story of Jewish people, we should recognize that the Jews are a microcosm of all humanity. How God revealed His character to the Jews is going to be consistent with how God

---

[1] The same statement about God's goodness and enduring love also appears several other times in the Bible: 1 Chr. 16:34; 2 Chr. 5:13, 7:3; Ps. 100:5, 107:1, 118:1,29, 136:1; Jer. 33:11.
[2] Variants of these statements are found in Neh. 9:17; Ps. 86:15, 103:8, 145:8; Joel 2:13; Jon. 4:2.

acts toward people in general—at least that is what Christians believe because of our faith in the message of the New Testament.

So let's examine in greater detail how God dealt with the Jews. The Old Testament tells that story: the selection of Abraham, Isaac, and Jacob as the patriarchal fathers of the people of Israel; the creation of the twelve tribes of Israel and a united loyalty to Moses and the Law he brought from Yahweh, the God of Israel; and the establishment of the Jewish nation-state with the rise of Hebrew kingship and Temple worship in Jerusalem. And then came the fall of Israel. The kings and people became increasingly corrupt and full of sin. To teach them a lesson for their sins, God imposed judgments on Israel in the form of war and exile. The Jewish nation was invaded and conquered by the Babylonians, and Jews were scattered in the Diaspora.

The eternal hell believer might want to stop there and say, "Aha! The fruit of sin is punishment, and that's that. Look what God did to the Jews when they transgressed His Law. No hope for them anymore." But that would be wrong. To the chagrin of fundamentalists who wish their theology could be so tidy, the Bible offers a promise of grace to sinful Israel. God is much more merciful than fundamentalists would have us believe. The same harsh Old Testament God who was full of fiery wrath when His people went astray would one day bring them back into the fold and into their divine inheritance they had squandered due to their own sins. The Bible promises reconciliation between God and His people and restoration of Israel after God's judgments come to a just and reasonable end.

Sure enough, after the Babylonian exile came the return of the Jews to reestablish the nation of Israel in the promised land. They rebuilt the Temple and resumed worshipping God in their holy city of Jerusalem. The pattern of sin, judgment, and salvation repeats itself over and over again in the historical story of the Jews.

In the prophetic books of the Bible, God describes Israel as an adulterous wife and a rebellious son. But He doesn't plan to divorce or disown His people. His judgments are temporary, not eternal and merciless. When Israel falls into sin, God says in anger, "she is not My wife, and I am not her husband. Let her remove the adulterous look from her face and the unfaithfulness from between her breasts." (Hos. 2:2). But God's forgiveness overpowers His anger, and after a time of separation and punishment for Israel, He says, "you will call Me 'my husband'; you will no longer call Me 'my master'.... I will betroth you to Me forever; I will betroth you in righteousness and justice, in love and compassion." (vs. 16,19). God's love is so great that He pledges to renew His vows with people who had violated His trust, broken His covenant, and turned away from Him to other gods.

God says to the people of Israel, "I reared children and brought them up, but they have rebelled against Me." (Isa. 1:2). They were "utterly estranged" from their divine Father (vs. 4 NRSV). God marvels at the punishments He had to inflict upon His children: "Why should you be beaten anymore? Why do you persist in rebellion? Your whole head is injured, your whole heart afflicted. From the sole of your foot to the top of your head there is no soundness—only wounds and welts and open sores... Your country is desolate, your cities burned with fire; your fields are being stripped by foreigners right before you..." (vss. 5-7). But all of these terrible judgments were only temporary, intended to set God's people back on the right track: "I will not accuse forever, nor will I always be angry, for then the spirit of man would grow faint before Me," says God. "I have seen his ways, but I will heal him; I will guide him and restore comfort to him..." (57:16,18). Moses tells us, "Know then in your heart that as a man disciplines his son, so the LORD your God disciplines you." (Deut. 8:5). The fatherly discipline and tough love of God was shown toward Israel when they became ensnared by sin and rebellion.

The Hebrew prophets often used hyperbole to describe God's anger and wrath toward His people Israel. Jeremiah, in particular, is known for his exaggerated rhetoric about divine judgment. He says that the fire of God's wrath against Jerusalem and Judah will not be quenched (Jer. 4:4, 7:20), that the city and nation will be smashed like a potter's jar that "cannot be repaired" (19:11), and that God's anger will burn forever (17:4). He says to his fellow Hebrews, "This is what the LORD says: 'Your wound is incurable, your injury beyond healing. There is no one to plead your cause, no remedy for your sore, no healing for you.'" (30:12-13). Sound familiar? That's some of the same kind of rhetoric used by fundamentalist Christian preachers who teach eternal hell. But even Jeremiah spoke of a merciful God. In the very same chapter where the supposedly "incurable" sins of Israel are mentioned, he also says, "'I am with you and will save you,' declares the LORD" (vs. 11), and "'I will restore you to health and heal your wounds,' declares the LORD." (vs. 17). This prophet was obviously very conflicted about his view of God's judgments! One minute he declares that things are utterly hopeless for Israel, and the next he promises restoration. The facts tell the true story. Israel was indeed restored, as history shows.

This passage in the Book of Jeremiah sums up God's attitude rather nicely: "'Return, faithless Israel,' declares the LORD, 'I will frown on you no longer, for I am merciful,' declares the LORD, 'I will not be angry forever. … How gladly would I treat you like sons and give you a desirable land, the most beautiful inheritance of any nation. I thought you would call Me "Father" and not turn away from following Me. But like a woman unfaithful to her husband, so you have been unfaithful to Me, O house of Israel,' declares the LORD. … 'Return, faithless people; I will cure you of backsliding.'" (3:12,19-20,22).

Calvinists argue that God will not deal with each individual human being in the same way God deals with Israel. *Calvinism* is the idea that some people are given unmerited grace by God, destined for forgiveness and salvation, whereas other people are destined for damnation because God has predetermined that they are never to be forgiven. This idea, in various forms, is popular among some of the more conservative Christians, because it enables fundamentalists to wriggle out of the problem of how God could be more merciful to Israel—promising ultimate reconciliation and restoration no matter how much they sin as a nation—while condemning some individuals to eternal hell according to fundamentalist doctrine.[3]

The problem with Calvinism is that the Bible teaches that "God does not show favoritism" for Jews over Gentiles (Rom. 2:11). If God is willing to save Israel no matter what, then His impartiality and consistency of character should mean that He is willing to save all people no matter what. So, many fundamentalists instead prefer to teach that

---

[3] The term Calvinism traditionally has been used to refer to the theological system of Protestant reformer John Calvin (1509-1564), who emphasized the "total depravity" of man and predestination of some people to heaven and others to hell, not based on their own spiritual worth or good works but on God's favor alone. Today, strict Calvinism is on the decline; but the key idea that God practices favoritism, giving some people more chance to be saved than others, remains a strong feature of the theology of many Christians.

God offers the *possibility* of forgiveness and salvation to all people impartially, but once a person's physical body dies, that hope is lost for those who died without repenting of their sins and accepting Christ. We will address the issue of salvation after death later. First, let's look at how the idea called *Arminianism*[4]—that salvation is all up to us according to our free will alone, each person fully and individually responsible for his own eternal fate—stacks up against the teachings of Jesus.

Divine Grace and the Parables of the Lost Sheep and the Lost Coin

Grace is an important Biblical concept which plays a role in the process of salvation. Grace means divine favor that is not deserved, but offered as a *free gift*. Jesus teaches us something about God's willingness to show grace to all people in the parable of the Lost Sheep. In this story, Jesus describes a shepherd who loses one out of a hundred of his sheep. When the sheep wanders off, straying from the flock and the way of the shepherd, he goes to look for it until he finds it. It is not the sheep that finds its way back to the shepherd on its own, but it is the benevolent action of the shepherd that enables the sheep to be saved from its lost condition.

Grace plays a role in salvation because God is greater than humans, as a shepherd is greater than sheep. Sometimes only God knows the way, and we cannot find it unless He comes to us first. God must take the first step, in order for the salvation process to proceed. But what about repentance? Isn't it necessary that we repent of our sins, by our own will and decision, so that we can return to God's way? Yes, but in the parable of the Lost Sheep, once the poor sheep who has lost sight of the flock sees its loving shepherd coming to the rescue, the sheep automatically turns around and resumes following the shepherd back to the flock—it is only natural. Remember that repentance means to turn around, to change course and begin going in the right direction. So the lost sheep (which represents a sinner) is in some sense brought to "repentance" simply by the act of the shepherd searching and find-

---

[4] Arminianism is the view of salvation developed by Dutch theologian Jacobus Arminius (1560-1609), which has become the mainstream view of most Protestants. It is based on the teaching that God allows people ultimately to refuse to be saved, because of their free will to choose unbelief and eternal hell over faith and eternal life in heaven.

ing the sheep. It is grace that makes this possible, not any effort on the part of the one that was lost.

Jesus says that God (the shepherd) is not satisfied with losing even one out of a hundred sheep (people). Anytime even one soul is lost, God will seek it and find it. So how could this God proclaimed by Jesus Christ send millions and millions of people to suffer in hell forever? That would be like the Divine Shepherd refusing to search out and find the lost sheep among His human family. As Jesus says, "your Father in heaven is not willing that any of these little ones should be lost." (Mat. 18:14). Every time He reaches out to a sinner and that sinner repents, God joyfully says, "Rejoice with me; I have found my lost sheep." (Luke 15:6). It is in God's benevolent character to keep looking until *everyone* who is lost is found, and in our salvation God takes great joy and pleasure.

Even though Jesus was sent in his earthly incarnation to bring grace and salvation specifically to sinners among the Jews, to "the lost sheep of Israel" (Mat. 15:24), he assures us that "I have other sheep that are not of this sheep pen. I must bring them also. They too will listen to my voice, and there shall be one flock and one shepherd." (John 10:16). God treats the Gentiles the same way as the Jews; He is in the process of saving *all* the lost sheep of the whole world.

Jesus shares another parable about the role of grace in salvation, the parable of the Lost Coin. "Suppose a woman has ten silver coins and loses one," says Jesus. "Does she not light a lamp, sweep the house and search carefully until she finds it? And when she finds it, she calls her friends and neighbors together and says, 'Rejoice with me; I have found my lost coin.' In the same way, I tell you, there is rejoicing in the presence of the angels of God over one sinner who repents." (Luke 15:8-10). Notice that a sinner in this story is represented by the symbol of a lost coin. The coin automatically "repents" when it is found by the woman. So we can be sure that God's grace is so powerful that repentance—and thus salvation—is guaranteed to occur when God searches for and finds one who is lost in sin.

Most important of all, we know from both of these parables that God *never* gives up, and He is never satisfied to lose *even one* person to sin. That doesn't sound like the fundamentalist "gospel" of eternal hell for ever-screaming millions.

The Fatherhood of God and the Parable of the Prodigal Son

One of the best known and most moving parables told by Jesus is the story of the Prodigal Son. In this parable, a young man demands his share of the inheritance from his father so that he can go off and start his own life apart from his family. He leaves for a distant land where he squanders all his money in wild living. Then comes a famine in the country, and he finds himself starving and seeking the food of pigs. He realizes how irresponsible he has been, and decides to go back to his father's house and ask to work as a mere hired servant so that he can eat. He believes that his father will never forgive him and will regard him as unworthy to be part of the family again.

The disobedient son underestimated the grace and forgiveness of his father. As he was returning home, "while he was still a long way off, his father saw him and was filled with compassion for him; he ran to his son, threw his arms around him and kissed him. The son said to him, 'Father, I have sinned against heaven and against you. I am no longer worthy to be called your son.' But the father said to his servants, 'Quick! Bring the best robe and put it on him. Put a ring on his finger and sandals on his feet. Bring the fattened calf and kill it. Let's have a feast and celebrate. For this son of mine was dead and is alive again; he was lost and is found.'" (Luke 15:20-24).

The sinner in this parable is the son who left home and wasted his inheritance on a corrupt lifestyle, before repenting, returning, and being blessed with his father's forgiveness. The father of course is God. But there is also another character in the story: the Prodigal Son's older brother, who stayed at home and dutifully obeyed the father all the time. He gets angry when the father is willing to forgive the sins of his irresponsible younger brother who came crawling back home in shame. "When this son of yours who has squandered your property with prostitutes comes home, you kill the fattened calf for him!" he cries to the father in fury (vs. 30). The father has to explain to him how willing he is to forgive, because his son has repented of his sins—and this is a cause for celebration, not further judgment.

Who does the unmerciful older brother represent in this parable? It is the harsh religious fundamentalists, who are never satisfied with God's limited judgment but always demand more and more vindictive retribution, a never-ending wrath without hope of forgiveness.

In Jesus' time and religious tradition, the fundamentalists were called *Pharisees*—and Jesus was always preaching against their arrogant and judgmental attitudes! The Gospels are full of stories of Jesus mocking the wrathful, self-righteous religiosity of the Pharisees and people who thought like them.

In the parable of the Prodigal Son, Jesus was making the point that God is like a loving, compassionate father, who is always willing to forgive us when we make a mistake and are willing to admit it and change direction. Unlike earthly, imperfect fathers who in some cases might disown their rebellious children and never be willing to reconcile with them, God "our Father in heaven" (Mat. 6:9) is better than that. He is so good that He would never, under any circumstances, disown us and condemn us forever. The possibility of reconciliation is always available—never to be withdrawn. Even while a sinner is still "a long way off," as in the parable of the Prodigal Son, as long as the child of God has decided to return to the Father, He is guaranteed to be "filled with compassion for him" and will celebrate his return and spiritual rebirth. Repentance on our part *always* produces forgiveness on God's part. That's because God is the perfect Father.

Jesus tells us these words of hope about our relationship with God: "Ask and it will be given to you; seek and you will find; knock and the door will be opened to you. For everyone who asks receives; he who seeks finds; and to him who knocks, the door will be opened. Which of you, if his son asks for bread, will give him a stone? Or if he asks for a fish, will give him a snake? If you, then, though you are evil, know how to give good gifts to your children, how much more will your Father in heaven give good gifts to those who ask Him!" (Mat. 7:7-11). Even an "evil" father may be willing to treat his own children well, especially when they please him. God is good and will remain compassionate toward His wayward children, because forbearance, forgiveness and mercy are in His very nature. These characteristics were demonstrated by Jesus Christ, who encouraged us to live the same way. Jesus says that "If your brother sins, rebuke him, and if he repents, forgive him. If he sins against you seven times in a day, and seven times comes back to you and says, 'I repent,' forgive him." (Luke 17:3-4). He commands us to forgive each other even up to "seventy-seven times." (Mat. 18:22). Surely God, who is infinitely

superior to us, could not do any less Himself! As soon as we are willing to ask for His forgiveness, seek Him out, and knock on the door of
heaven, He will be there.

The door will always remain open. Whenever we are ready to
exit the hell of sin and return to our Father's house, we will find Him
standing there waiting for us, with arms wide open, ready to embrace
us in joyful reconciliation. Unlike the older brother in the parable of
the Prodigal Son, who is like religious fundamentalists who want God
to be harsh and unforgiving to some of our brothers and sisters in
the human family, the real God is infinitely more loving and compassionate and would not leave any of us outside His door in the hell of
permanent judgment.

Jesus' Teaching of Gehenna

Now that we have seen a few Biblical reasons to believe in the ultimate reconciliation of all people, we should examine some teachings
in the Bible that seem to argue for a burning hell where some will experience terrible punishments for their sins. First of all, let me be clear
about one thing: hell is real. The Bible teaches in many places that sinners must experience judgment, and this is described in terms that do
not sound like fun. Fire, worms, weeping and gnashing of teeth. Yes,
those things are indeed in the Bible, as much as we might prefer it to
be otherwise. Jesus himself spoke of such horrors. So we cannot simply
ignore the Bible verses that seem to support a traditional fundamentalist view of damnation. But do we really understand these verses, or
have we been led astray by false and misleading interpretations?

Fundamentalists love to remind people that the "worm does not
die, and the fire is not quenched" in hell (Mark 9:48). They often quote
such passages with relish, with a gleam of zealous wrath in their eye,
longing to see sinners' flesh roasting with fire and crawling with gi-
gantic worms that will eat your innards over and over again. They talk
about how God will "throw them into the fiery furnace, where there
will be weeping and gnashing of teeth" (Mat. 13:50) from the occupants
of hell, like the cries and shrieks of prisoners being tortured in a medieval dungeon. Oh, the pain of hell must be so intense, the fundamentalists impress upon us, that it would be better that you cut off your hand
or gouge out your eyeball if it causes you to sin, rather than to enter hell

(see Mat. 18:8-9). However, the actual word that is used in the original Greek Bible for "hell" in these passages, and pretty much wherever else Jesus referred to it, is *Gehenna*. This word had a specific meaning to the minds of ancient Jews—a meaning which has been forgotten by many Christians today. It does not mean a literal place of torture with fire and worms that people will suffer in the afterlife for all eternity.

No, Gehenna to Jesus and his ancient Jewish audience had a very different meaning. It was a reference to a valley outside Jerusalem where children had been sacrificed in fire to the Canaanite god Molech. God said of this barbaric and evil practice, "I never commanded, nor did it enter My mind, that they should do such a detestable thing." (Jer. 32:35). If God didn't want people to destroy their children with fire, surely He would not do this to His own children—human beings—in a fiery eternal torture chamber beyond the grave. It would be absurd to think that God holds mere humans to a higher moral standard than His own divine perfection!

Jesus' use of the term Gehenna to refer to impending divine judgment was actually directed more at the nation of Israel than individual people. Like the prophets of the Old Testament who warned of judgments from God upon a sinful nation, usually in the form of military defeat, exile, or famine and pestilence, Jesus was issuing a prophetic call for Israel to repent or else face destructive divine judgment. He often referred to himself as the "son of man," a term used in the Hebrew scriptures to refer to prophets associated with apocalypse. He predicted that the city of Jerusalem and its great Temple would be destroyed: "Do you see these great buildings? Not one stone will be left here upon another; all will be thrown down." (Mark 13:2 NRSV). He said that the people of Judea must "flee to the mountains" (Mat. 24:16) to avoid being killed in the time of tribulation that was soon coming. Jesus used graphic imagery of a hated, shameful place called Gehenna to make it clear to the Jews what their fate would be if they did not turn back to the Lord and away from their sins. Jesus was, after all, sent to the Jews, and their nation had become very corrupt in the time of Roman occupation. He was hoping to save them from destruction by increasing their righteousness, which would bring divine blessing.

The Jews did not repent, and history records that Roman armies utterly destroyed the nation of Israel in 70 C.E., including the Temple in accordance with the prophetic words of Jesus. Many thousands of Jews were slaughtered and their corpses were, in fact, literally thrown into the valley called Gehenna to rot and burn. So in one sense, Jesus' prophecy of people going to Gehenna was fulfilled literally. To have one's body left exposed and eaten as carrion instead of receiving a proper burial was a sign of great shame and indignity in the eyes of the Jews. Such a death was itself seen as a terrible punishment from God, regardless of any considerations of the afterlife.

In another, more symbolic sense, Gehenna was also used by Jesus to represent the judgment of God upon sinners in general, which is a judgment of cleansing and destruction. If a person is "sent to Gehenna," this means going into a place or state of being in which God is working to destroy the garbage in one's life and in one's soul. This could happen either in this life on earth or in the life hereafter. Just like the Prodigal Son found himself one day wallowing with the pigs as a consequence of his sins, someone who goes to "Gehenna" is in a state of judgment where they can finally see where their corrupt actions have brought them. For some people, such an unpleasant judgment is the only way they will ever see the need to repent.

Like Sodom and Gomorrah which we have already learned are someday to be restored by God according to the prophet Ezekiel, Gehenna is also to be made holy again according to Jeremiah. "The days are coming, declares the Lord, when... The whole valley where dead bodies and ashes are thrown [Gehenna]... will be holy to the Lord." (Jer. 31:38,40). This can be taken to have both a literal and a metaphorical meaning. Today, the valley of Gehenna is verdant parkland in the modern city of Jerusalem. Similarly, it is reasonable to believe that even as Jesus used Gehenna in a symbolic way, Jeremiah's prophecy of the restoration of Gehenna to a state of holiness refers not only to the literal place on earth that has been purified and redeemed, but also the eventual end of suffering for sinners as part of God's plan for the redemption of all. Jesus, who was thoroughly familiar with the Hebrew scriptures, would have known of this prophecy when he used the imagery of Gehenna. Therefore, implicit in every reference Jesus made to a soul going to Gehenna is the idea that the state of corruption is not permanent, but even those who were cast out into Gehenna will someday again be "holy to the Lord."

Praise God that nothing, no matter how evil, is beyond His power to restore to goodness! Even Sodom and Gehenna, the two places in the Bible associated with the greatest evil, are prophesied to be restored and made new after being judged by God and brought down to utter shame and contempt. Such amazing prophecies reveal the Biblical God's character as a God of universal salvation, not eternal damnation for anyone or anything.

God in Hell: The Hidden Meaning of Fire and Brimstone

Many Christians think they can completely avoid the fires of hell. If they confess Christ, they will instantly go to a blissful paradise when they die, but those who were not Christian during their life on earth will find themselves in an everlasting place of torment in the afterlife.

This simplistic vision of a binary universe—some people never tasting the fires of hell and other people immersed in the agonizing fires of God's wrath forever—is a doctrine that can only be supported by ignoring certain teachings of the Bible. The truth is, *everybody* is going to get some fire, and nobody will be left in the fire after it has served its purpose. Jesus says that "everyone will be salted with fire" (Mark 9:49), a phrase that suggests that the application of divine judgment is a good thing, designed for improvement and benefit of a person's spirit even though it may be temporarily painful.

God Himself *is* fire. Many verses in the Bible attest to this. "God is a consuming fire…" (Deut. 4:24). When Isaiah was called by God, an angel put a fiery coal on his lips as a symbol of purification, saying to the new prophet, "See, this has touched your lips; your guilt is taken away and your sin atoned for." (Isa. 6:7). This coal of fire on his mouth signified that Isaiah had been made ready to speak the message of the Lord—the fire from God was to take away Isaiah's sin and make him holy. The Holy Spirit, which is one form or persona of God, is described as coming to the apostles as "tongues of fire" resting upon their heads (Acts 2:3), giving them powers of divine inspiration and prophecy. Baptism in the Holy Spirit is a baptism of fire, and this spiritual rebirth is a good thing that all people are called to attain.

But fire is difficult and unpleasant to go through, as long as there is something for it to burn. If one's soul is still sinful, mortal, in a sense "combustible," we will suffer pain and loss when God's fire touches us.

John the Baptist said that Jesus "will baptize you with the Holy Spirit and with fire. His winnowing fork is in his hand, and he will clear his threshing floor, gathering his wheat into the barn and burning up the chaff with unquenchable fire." (Mat. 3:11-12). As Paul wrote, "the fire" of God's judgment "will test the quality of each man's work. If what he has built survives, he will receive his reward. If it is burned up, he will suffer loss; he himself will be saved, but only as one escaping through the flames." (1 Cor. 3:13-14).

In the original New Testament, the same Greek word for fire (*puros*) is used to describe the fire of the Holy Spirit and the fire of hell. The purpose of the "fires" (divine trials and tests) of "hell" (judgment) is so that God can *transform* us through His judgment, burning away our sinful nature and replacing it with a more perfect, Christlike nature. Fire is an apt metaphor for this transformative process that leads to salvation, because literal fire is a physical process that causes matter to change its form and become something else. When fire is applied to matter, it will burn if it is combustible (that is, capable of being changed into a different form). Whatever is not combustible will remain unchanged. Sinners will experience the presence of God and His work in their life as a raging fire that will burn much, while saints will experience God's fire as a light that cannot harm them, because the saintly soul has already been changed in the fires of judgment and no longer "burns" (suffers judgment) when touched by the divine.

The Bible uses the metaphor of refining valuable metals in fire to get rid of the impurities within, as a description of how the fire of God transforms people and perfects them. When the Lord judges people, He "will be like a refiner's fire or a launderer's soap. He will sit as a refiner and purifier of silver..." (Mal. 3:2-3). So hell is like a washing machine for a dirty soul, and like a furnace where bad parts are removed from us and we come out shining like perfect silver. The slavery of the Jews in Egypt before the exodus was described by Moses as "the iron-smelting furnace" (Deut. 4:20), indicating that God puts people through times of suffering as a way of testing them and shaping them, preparing them for a greater spiritual inheritance. As the Apostle Peter says, trials come to us so that our faith, which is "of greater worth than gold," may be "refined by fire" and "proved genuine." (1 Pet. 1:7).

In metallurgy, a precious metal such as gold or silver can be puri-fied by the use of fire: the base metals (impurities) contained within are eliminated when fire is applied, enabling the gold or silver to be refined to a greater quality. Similarly, the divine fire of judgment rep-resents the process of changing a person, destroying or separating out any parts of one's character that are not compatible with a perfect spiri-tual nature that is in harmony with God. After the burning or refining process of judgment, a person's impurities (sins) are reduced or elimi-nated, and what remains of the person is greater in God's sight than it was before, while it was contaminated by sin. The thoroughly puri-fied person reaches a point where the divine fire has no effect, because there is no longer anything bad to burn; the person's spirit attains the incombustible state of salvation.

Fundamentalists like to use descriptions of the "lake of fire and brim-stone" in the Book of Revelation as evidence that some people will suffer a ferocious torture from God for all eternity. They envision this lake as a place of molten lava where the souls of sinners and nonbelievers will writhe and scream in agony forever, tossed to and fro in the liquid fire of God's wrath. Whether the Lake of Fire is literal or spiritual doesn't neces-sarily matter to them; the point is, they see it as an instrument of torture and a state of being wholly removed from God's presence. Hell, to funda-mentalists, is the complete absence of God. The pain of sinners in hell is because of God's abandonment of them in a place deprived of all that is good and filled with all that is evil.

However, this view of the Lake of Fire and Brimstone is the ex-act opposite of what this vivid metaphor in the Bible was intended to convey. We have already seen that the fire of hell and the fire of God's very being is the same thing: *puros*. And guess what? The brimstone (sulfur) that is in the Lake of Fire also means the presence of God! In Greek, the language of the New Testament, the word for sulfur is *thei-on*, which means divine incense and comes from the same root as the word for God. Burning brimstone was regarded as having the power to purify and ward off disease. The Lake of Fire and Brimstone (puros and theion) is therefore a place in which sinners come in direct, inti-mate contact with God and His power to destroy the sin within us and heal us of its detrimental effects. It is a place of purgatorial punishment that serves a beneficial purpose. Its goal is to transform the sinner to the point where being in the presence of God no longer is painful, but joyful. Instead of experiencing God as a tormenting lake of fire, the repentant sinner who has attained salvation experiences God as the Holy Spirit infusing one's being with the nature and essence of holiness.

So the "lake of fire and brimstone" is one way of being baptized in the Holy Spirit, born again the hard way by experiencing the full-blown judgment of God. It is certainly not the most pleasant way to be saved, but God doesn't give up on anyone—even those who require severe trials and penalties before they can be set free of their sins. The bottom line is, some people get more fire than others, because some people require more attention from God in order to be changed. Some people only need to be "salted" with fire, while others will need a whole "lake" of fire to find salvation.

The true meaning of the metaphorical language in the Book of Revelation about the Lake of Fire can be more easily understood when we consider this verse: "Then death and Hades [hell] were thrown into the lake of fire. The lake of fire is the second death." (Rev. 20:14). This is a prophecy that someday, at the end of time, death and hell will both die (be destroyed). In other words, no one will be permanently annihilated or tormented forever, because that would be the continuation of death or hell. The only other possibility is that God will save all people—neither annihilating the wicked nor condemning them to an eternal state of pain. Universal reconciliation is the only way death and hell can cease to exist, which is what the Bible promises us in the often misunderstood metaphor of the Lake of Fire.

Biblical Word Games: "Eternal Punishment"?

Much of the confusion about hell in Christianity is because of a pervasive mistranslation of a key word in the Bible. Believe it or not, *one word* can change an entire religion, turning a positive message into something very negative. This word is *aionios*, which is found in many places in the original Greek New Testament. Aionios means "age-lasting" or "lasting for an age, an indefinite period of time." But it gets translated in all popular versions of the Bible as "eternal" or "everlasting." Unfortunately, this is the word used throughout the New Testament to refer to the duration of punishment in hell.

It is clear that aionios in Biblical Greek did not mean an infinite length of time. We can be certain of this because there was a different word in that language for eternal, the word *aidios*. This word was never used in the Bible to refer to hell. It was, however, used by Paul to describe the "*eternal* power and divine nature" of God (Rom. 1:20). The authors of the scriptures could have chosen to describe hell as aidios, but they never did—and that deliberate omission says a lot. Aionios is the root from which we derive the English word eon, meaning a long period of time. It is not the same thing as eternity. No matter how long an eon might be, there is an infinite difference!

In various Greek writings of the ancient world—both by Christians and non-Christians—the correct usage of aionios is shown. It often was used to refer to the duration of a man's life or a period of up to 1000 years, rarely longer, and never to eternity. Consider these examples from the first few centuries of the Christian Era:

> "Upon a lead tablet found in the Necropolis at Adrumetum in the Roman province of Africa, near Carthage, the following inscription, belonging to the early third century, is scratched in Greek: 'I am adjuring Thee, the great God, the eonian, and more than eonian (*epaionion*) and almighty...' If by eonian, endless time were meant, then what could be more than endless time? In the *Apostolical Constitutions*, a work of the fourth century A.D., it is said, *kai touto humin esto nomimon aionion hos tes suntleias to aionos*, 'And let this be to you an eonian ordinance until the consummation of the eon.' Obviously there was no thought in the author's mind of endless time. ... [First-century Roman historian] Josephus shows that *aionios* did not mean endlessness, for he uses it of the period between the giving of the law to Moses and that of his own writing; to the period of the imprisonment of the tyrant John by the Romans; and to the period during which Herod's temple stood. The temple had already been destroyed by the time Josephus was writing. St. Gregory of Nyssa speaks of *aionios diastêma*, 'an eonian interval.' It would be absurd to call an interval 'endless.' St. Chrysostum,

in his homily on Eph. 2:1-3, says that 'Satan's kingdom is æonian; that is, it will cease with the present world.' St. Justin Martyr repeatedly used the word *aionios* as in the Apol. (p. 57), *aionion kolasin ...all ouchi chiliontaetê periodon*, 'eonian chastening ...but a period, not a thousand years.' Or, as some translate the last clause: 'but a period of a thousand years only.' He limits the eonian chastening to a period of a thousand years, rather than to endlessness."[5]

The problem started when the Bible was translated into Latin. Aionios was rendered as the Latin word *aeternus*, meaning eternal. This was based on the proclamation of the Roman Emperor Justinian in 544 C.E. that hell lasts forever. He described it in Greek as *ateleutetos* (another word meaning "endless"), rather than aionios. He knew—as everyone did at the time—that the Greek word aionios did not itself mean never-ending, so he had to use a different word that was not used by the authors of the Bible in order to insert the doctrine of endless punishments into Christianity. The legacy of this error has lasted for centuries and done untold damage to the Christian faith.

One of the most well known examples of this mistranslation is Mat. 25:46. Fundamentalists always like to point to this verse as supposed confirmation of the idea that hell is eternal torment. They open their Bible and read that Jesus said that sinners "will go away to eternal punishment, but the righteous to eternal life." But is this *really* what Jesus said in this verse? When we look at what it says in the original Greek, we find that Jesus spoke of *aionios kolasis*, which means age-lasting chastisement, not eternal punishment.

The word *kolasis* has the connotation of beneficial disciplinary correction, such as a parent might punish a child for wrongdoing with the purpose of reform. This is in sharp contrast to *timoria*, meaning punitive or vindictive punishment. Kolasis comes from a root word meaning "to prune," as a tree or plant. When a gardener prunes, it is not done to torture the vegetation, but to remove dead or crooked branches and cause it to grow in a better, more beautiful way. Pruning

---

[5] Abbott, Louis. *An Analytical Study of Words*. Chapter 9. Available online at http://www.members.cox.net/tmurr10/aswundivided.html and http://www.tentmaker.org/books/asw/index.html

is actually an important horticultural technique to improve the quality and increase the yield of fruit-bearing trees and vines. So God is going to prune the souls of sinners, cutting away the parts that are corrupted by sin, in order to transform the person into a more holy and fruitful son or daughter of God. Kolasis is loving, parental discipline with the goal of helping the one being subjected to it. That's a far cry from the fundamentalist doctrine of damnation! Aionios kolasis should not be translated as "eternal punishment," but should be understood to mean a limited period of time in which a person will receive divine judgment for reformation and improvement of character. If Matthew had meant to suggest that Jesus taught eternal torment, he probably would have written *aidios timoria*.

Does "eternal life" (Greek: aionios zoe) in Mat. 25:46 and similar verses mean that our life with God in heaven only lasts for an age, just like the limited term some souls will spend in hell? No. Even though the word used here is aionios, the same word to describe the duration of hell, that does not mean the heavenly life is mortal or perishable. We can be sure that the life in heaven is eternal because of the following verse in the Bible: "When the perishable has been clothed with the imperishable, and the mortal with immortality, then the saying that is written will come true: 'Death has been swallowed up in victory.'" (1 Cor. 15:54). This is referring to the life of the resurrection. The Greek words translated as "imperishable" (*aphtharsia*) and "immortality" (*athanasia*) really do mean what they say in English. So the point Jesus was making in verses like Mat. 25:46 is that sinners will spend a period of time being judged and corrected by God—the aionian chastisement, surely not a pleasant process—while righteous people will be enjoying the blessings of God, the aionian life in Christ. Eventually, everyone will be reconciled and redeemed and will live eternally in heaven, but before that happens, some will receive judgments for an age while others are receiving rewards.

Many versions of the Bible also mistranslate other words in reference to the duration of hell. One such word is the Hebrew *olam*, used in the Old Testament. For example, in the legend of Jonah and the fish, the Bible says that the prophet Jonah was swallowed up and remained inside the belly of the great fish for an "olam" period of time, which was three days. However, Bible versions erroneously translate

Jon. 2:6 to say that he was in the fish "forever"—despite the fact that it says in 1:17 that he was there for only three days. Olam can mean any indeterminate period of time, in this case three days. But for some strange reason, most Bible translations translate it as "forever" even when it doesn't make sense for it to mean forever.

Perhaps this is because of poetic license and exaggeration. When people are in dire straights—such as being swallowed by a whale or being sent to hell—they will tend to overestimate the length of time they had to endure in such a terrible circumstance. Three days in a hellish condition could seem to last forever. Perhaps that's the point many translators of the Bible are trying to make when they describe Jonah's three days in the fish as lasting "forever." Obviously, it is not literally true. The Bible is full of such exaggeration for effect, and translators may make the exaggerations even more extreme through their choice of words. We need to recognize this when we consider the issue of hell. If hell is olam or aionios, it might feel like a long time and we might even poetically describe it as "forever"—but it is *not really* forever!

Let's look at how Jonah felt when he was in the belly of the fish. He said, "In my distress I called to the LORD, and He answered me. From the depths of the grave [Hebrew: Sheol] I called for help, and You listened to my cry. You hurled me into the deep, into the very heart of the seas, and the currents swirled about me; all Your waves and breakers swept over me. I said, 'I have been banished from Your sight; yet I will look again toward Your holy temple.'... [T]he earth beneath barred me in forever. But You brought my life up from the pit, O LORD my God." (Jon. 2:1-4,6).

This must be what it feels like to be in hell. One is filled with despair, thinking that one has been forever abandoned by God in a turbulent sea of trouble. But then, one cries out to God for help in repentance, and God will respond by bringing one back from "the pit." What a perfect example of God's mercy to sinners! When it seems like all hope is lost, God is ready to rescue us, and will do so without fail. Like Jonah who escaped death in the belly of the whale, sinners may go through an olam or aionios period of distress—God only knows how long—but will emerge from the experience having confronted their sins and the consequences, and returning to God because of the trials they had to endure.

Before we move on, we should quickly point out that there are several different words in the original languages of the Bible that are translated as "hell" in some Bible versions. We have already discussed Gehenna. There is also *Sheol*, which we have mentioned in passing. This Hebrew word does not necessarily mean a place of torment, but is simply the underworld, the shadowy abode of all the dead according to ancient Judaism. This fact has not prevented some Bible translations—most noteworthy being the perennially popular King James version—from blatantly mistranslating this word as "hell" in some verses, causing a great deal of confusion. There is also the Greek word *Hades*, used in the New Testament to refer both to the world of the dead in general, and also in some cases more specifically to the sinful dead. *Tartarus* appears only once in the Bible (2 Pet. 2:4), referring to a temporary place of confinement for fallen angels awaiting further judgment by God. *In no case* are any of these places said to be permanent, eternal, or never-ending states of being, in the original untranslated text of the Bible.

The bottom line is that Bible translators have tried very hard to make the Bible say that hell lasts forever, but a careful study of the languages in which it was written reveals the truth. "Eternal torment" is simply not Biblical. It is an invention of church tradition that became established in the mass consciousness of Christianity because of centuries of faulty Bible translations.

Why Jesus Went to Hell

There are several other Biblical reasons to believe in universal reconciliation rather than eternal damnation. One of them is that Jesus himself said that all people will eventually be saved. When talking to his disciples about his death on the cross and why he must be crucified, Jesus said, "I, when I am lifted up from the earth, will draw all men to myself." (John 12:32). How is that going to happen? How can Jesus, after he has died, been resurrected, and left this earth, continue to draw people to himself? And more importantly, how can he claim to draw *all* people to himself? He did say all people—not some, but all. That includes the living and the dead, the righteous and the sinners, the Jews and the Gentiles, the Christians and the non-Christians. Everyone is included in Jesus' promise.

Unless Jesus plans to spend eternity in hell, it is safe to conclude that drawing all people to himself means drawing all into heaven. Many people who die do not go straight to heaven; that much is clear, according to Jesus' own teachings. When Jesus was alive on earth, he went to those who needed the saving grace of God the most: the lost sheep of Israel, the sinners and outcasts. Jesus violated Jewish tradition by eating and fellowshipping with such undesirable people and showed them God's unconditional love, infuriating popular religious leaders of his day. Is it not logical to conclude, based on what we already know Jesus did for people on earth, that in the afterlife he would continue to go to the lost souls who most need God's help? In other words, Jesus would go to hell.

That's right, folks, instead of luxuriating in paradise with his Father, Jesus probably spends a lot of his time in the flames with the sinners, talking to them and encouraging them to repent and be released from hell. In our hearts, we just *know* that's what Jesus would do. For him, going to earth was itself like going to hell. And he promised that after being hung on a cross, he would continue to draw all people to himself. It was his death that actually made this possible! If Jesus had never died, he could not have gone to hell to reach the souls languishing there.

The main purpose of the crucifixion of Jesus Christ was to prove that God loves us so much that He was willing to become a man and die a horrible death, even the shameful death of a criminal, so that He could be resurrected and the power of sin can be defeated. It is through the cross of Christ that we see God's amazing, unfailing love for mankind. It is through the resurrection of Jesus Christ that we see that the powers of evil have already been overcome by God's omnipotent goodness. Jesus still lives, despite the best attempts of man and the forces of evil to kill him. Jesus is still actively saving souls, just as he did during his time on earth—and he will never stop working until *all souls* are redeemed and reconciled to God.

We needn't speculate about whether Jesus went to hell to save people there. If we trust the Bible, we can be certain of it. The Apostle Peter informs us that Jesus went and preached to suffering souls in the afterlife, after he had died on the cross. His sacrificial death would enable sinners to be released from punishment and reunited with God. "For Christ died for sins once for all, the righteous for the unrighteous, to bring you to God. He was put to death in the body but made alive in the spirit, through which also he went and preached to the spirits in prison who disobeyed long ago…" (1 Pet. 3:18-20). This is confirmation of Jesus' promise recorded in John 12:32 to draw all people to himself after leaving earth. Even in death, in the spirit world, unbelievers and sinners can still have an opportunity to be saved by hearing the message of Jesus Christ delivered to them.

Of course, fundamentalists argue that Peter meant to tell us that Jesus went to hell to laugh at its prisoners—not to release them by sharing the Good News of salvation for all people, but to inform them that he is saving some fortunate people but never them, just to add to their hopeless misery. But in making such an argument, they are going against the words of Peter, who said, "For this is the reason the Gospel was proclaimed even to the dead, so that, though they had been judged in the flesh as everyone is judged, they might live in the spirit as God does." (1 Pet. 4:6 NRSV). In other words, people who were judged for their earthly sins and went to hell can still have the opportunity to find true spiritual life with God beyond the grave. The drawing power of Jesus will win them over and allow them to find relief from God's judgments and enter into peace and reconciliation.

Just because somebody is physically dead does not mean the opportunity to hear the Gospel and be saved by it has forever passed them by. Paul seems to have shared Peter's view, saying that the Gospel is "proclaimed to every creature under heaven" (Col. 1:23). That certainly would include those in hell. Another reason we can be confident that post-mortem salvation was an original Christian belief is that Paul approvingly mentions baptism being performed on behalf of the dead in the Corinthian church (see 1 Cor. 15:29). This practice presupposes the idea that God will save even those who died in sin and unbelief.

How Paul Preached the Gospel

The greatest evangelist of the early church was undoubtedly the Apostle Paul. He wrote the largest portion of what we now know as the New Testament, and founded numerous churches from the eastern Mediterranean all the way to Rome. Paul, formerly Saul, was a hardcore Jewish fundamentalist who hated and persecuted Christians.

Then one day he saw the resurrected Christ on the road to Damascus and was struck blind for three days, until he found himself in the home of a Christian where he was baptized into the new faith. After that, he became zealous for the Gospel and devoted the rest of his life to spreading the message of Christ throughout the Roman Empire—suffering much in the process—and establishing it as a faith for all people, not only the Jews. If it weren't for Paul, his vision, travels and copious writings, Christianity might not have survived the first century and gone on to become a major world religion.

What is most noteworthy about the message Paul preached is the absence of one teaching that forms the basis of the message taught by today's fundamentalist Christians. That teaching is eternal hell—the danger of damnation for anyone who does not accept Jesus Christ as Lord and Savior. Paul never talked about that! In his sermons and letters, he *never* said anything like this: "Here is the Gospel: that Jesus died for your sins so that God doesn't have to send you to hell forever." But that is what many Christian preachers say today. Why couldn't they teach the faith more like Paul?

Paul understood that the Gospel was supposed to be a message of Good News. He did not go around scaring people by promising an endless torture unless they converted to his religion. That wouldn't be good news at all. Obviously, if Paul had believed in eternal hell, he would have talked about it—a lot. Paul was a sincere, serious Christian leader who wanted to save the world for Christ. But he never talked about saving people from eternal torment. Even if Paul had never said anything to reveal a belief in universal reconciliation, we could logically deduce that he believed all will eventually be saved.

The truth is, Paul actually did openly teach about his belief in the ultimate reconciliation of all people. Consider this remarkable statement: "Consequently, just as the result of one trespass was condemnation for all men, so also the result of one act of righteousness was justification that brings life for all men. For just as through the disobedience of the one man the many were made sinners, so also through the obedience of the one man the many will be made righteous." (Rom. 5:18-19). Note that the phrase "the many" refers to all human beings collectively, both in regard to the fall of man and the salvation of man. The sin of Adam caused all his descendents, the entire human race, to be predisposed to sin. The tendency of sinfulness is passed on in the genes. But the perfect righteousness of Jesus Christ enables all people, the entire human race, to be forgiven and transformed by God. Paul prophesies that this *will* happen, just as certainly as all became sinners through Adam, not through any choice of their own. That's because Christ is like the *new Adam*, the new pattern on which all people will be modeled. "Just as we have borne the likeness of the earthly man [Adam], so shall we bear the likeness of the man from heaven [Christ]." (1 Cor. 15:49).

Paul says that all people will someday recognize Jesus as Lord, and that this will be a glorious outcome of God's plan. He promises that "at the name of Jesus every knee should bow, in heaven and on earth and under the earth, and every tongue confess that Jesus Christ is Lord, to the glory of God the Father." (Phil. 2:10-11). This is not a prediction that all people will cry uncle and grudgingly accept Jesus as the Lord who forever condemns them to torture. Such a horrible outcome would not be to the glory of God. Also note that the word "should" in this translation means shall or will, not ought. The verse is saying that all knees *will* bow and all tongues *will* confess, not that they merely ought to. When they finally do, it will be in a way that glorifies God, which means a true acceptance of Jesus, forgiveness and reconciliation. We can be certain of this because Paul also says that "Everyone who calls on the name of the Lord will be saved." (Rom. 10:13). If every tongue will confess that Jesus is Lord, and everyone who does so is saved, that means everyone will be saved!

There are several other important passages in Paul's writings where he talks about the destiny of all people to be reconciled with God. Here is one that is particularly striking: "This is a trustworthy saying that deserves full acceptance (and for this we labor and strive), that we have put our hope in the living God, who is the Savior of all men, and especially of those who believe." (1 Tim. 4:9-10). He clearly states that God is saving all people, and that believers are *especially* saved right now. This corresponds to the idea of the "age-lasting life" that the righteous will enjoy while sinners are experiencing "age-lasting chastisement." In the end, all will be saved, but not everybody is saved at the same time. Some people must experience hell before they can be saved. Well, more accurately, all of us go through at least a little bit of fire on the way to salvation, but for some of us it's a like a sprinkle of salt, whereas for others it's like a pit of molten lava. It's whatever is necessary in each case.

We need not imagine God's judgment as so harsh that it never ends, to be sure that the universe is a place of justice where sin receives its due. Let's trust in the Biblical message of Jesus, Paul, and the other great authors of the Judeo-Christian scriptural tradition, who understood that sin requires judgment, but that the purpose of the judgments of God is for redemption and transformation, not eternal condemnation.

Overcoming Objections to Universal Reconciliation

Now that we have seen some of the basic arguments for universal reconciliation, we should consider some of the most common objections. In Part Two, we will answer several questions that are typically raised by fundamentalists and opponents of universalism, and we will show why these issues do not in any way hurt the case for an inclusive view of salvation. Some of these questions are undoubtedly serious stumbling blocks for people who are exploring Christian Universalism or would prefer not to believe in an eternal hell. Some are Biblical issues, and others are philosophical, experiential, or practical issues. In every case, the best attempts of proponents of damnationism to undermine Christian Universalism only serve to spark further beneficial examination of the Christian faith, leading to a deeper understanding of the true message of the Gospel, its foundations and its effects on our lives.

The True Meaning of the Cross—A Deeper Look at Atonement

Why did Jesus have to die on the cross if not to save us from eternal hell? This is probably the number one question asked by Christians who are skeptical that universal salvation could be compatible with Biblical Christianity. And it is perhaps the single most important question that Christian Universalists must answer if we are to successfully explain our view of the Gospel to sincere believers in Christ. Many Christians believe that Jesus' sacrificial death enables God to forgive the sins of those who believe in him, but those who do not hold the correct beliefs about Christ in this lifetime can never be forgiven and must eternally remain separated from God in hell. If there is no good reason why Jesus had to be crucified other than to allow people to escape damnation, then perhaps God really does condemn non-Christians to burn forever in the torments of hell.

Fortunately, there is a good reason for the cross of Christ other than what fundamentalists teach. And this alternative explanation is found in the Bible. The reason for the crucifixion of Jesus Christ is that it proves that God's love is unfailing and conquers all evil. The cross is not a dividing line, permanently excluding some people from the love of their Creator. No, the cross is a ladder to heaven through which all people may eventually return to the Father who sent His Son, the Lord Jesus, into our world. Because of the central importance of the crucifixion and resurrection of Jesus Christ in the Christian faith, we will examine this matter in some detail.

Before Jesus died on the cross and rose again from the grave, it was very difficult for people to believe in the goodness of God. People usually feared God and knew He was great and mighty, but did not necessarily love Him. God seemed to arbitrarily favor some people and not others, according to whim and caprice. When bad things happened, people thought God was punishing them or had abandoned them—they had no concept of a loving Father in heaven who cares about the welfare of each and every one of us and wants to save us through divine grace.

The disturbing implications of the ancient view of God as a graceless tyrant were explored in one of the most important books in the Bible, the Book of Job. As the story goes, Job was a righteous man who was tortured by the devil—with sicknesses and calamities one after another—so much that his whole life was ruined. God allowed this to happen and did not answer his prayers for help. His friends told him God must be against him and that he was accursed because of some secret sins he might have committed. Job rejected this explanation and struggled to understand the terrible and senseless things that were happening, but could not find any answer. Naturally, his spirit was crushed and he became angry at God.

Job was a righteous man as the Bible attests, but Jesus was far more righteous than Job. In fact, Jesus was the perfect saint, a man who never sinned at all. The Bible says that Jesus was tempted by the devil and completely resisted all his temptations to do wrong. Jesus started a ministry to feed the poor, heal the sick, and comfort the outcasts of society. He had miraculous powers to cure diseases and overcome evil powers. He announced that the promised Kingdom of God had come, and he was the King who would bring justice and peace to Israel and the world. Despite all this, God cut off Jesus' ministry before he could turn his vision into reality. God chose to allow Jesus to suffer and die a death of torture on the cross.

No wonder most people thought Jesus was a fraud! He was executed in a grotesque and agonizing way—a death of utter humiliation and degradation reserved only for the most heinous criminals. Perhaps Jesus was cursed by God. If God really loved and approved of him, why didn't He prevent the crucifixion? Would God allow this to happen to the true Messiah?

Yes, even God's own Son could be treated unfairly by fate. That was part of the plan all along. Isaiah's prophecy of the suffering Messiah says that God's chosen one would be "despised and rejected by men, a man of sorrows, and familiar with suffering." (Isa. 53:3). He would be "pierced for our transgressions" and "crushed for our iniquities," and "by his wounds we are healed." (vs. 5). What does this really mean? Does it mean that if Jesus had not been nailed to a cross, God could not have forgiven any human beings of their sins, and everyone would have had to spend eternity in hell?

Just because Jesus' death is regarded as similar to an Old Testament animal sacrifice does not mean God is inherently unwilling or unable to forgive our sins without the spilling of blood. God is omnipotent and can forgive anyone at any time, if He chooses to do so. Jesus said, "Your Father is merciful" (Luke 6:36), and the Apostle John said, "God is love" (1 John 4:16)—so we know that forgiveness and compassion are in God's nature. Jesus forgave a woman caught in the act of adultery, and he even asked God to forgive the Roman soldiers who pounded nails into his hands! The notion of Jesus as a sacrificial lamb is a metaphor, particularly useful for ancient Jews who were familiar with slaughtering animals in the temple as a way to atone for their sins.

We must realize that even in Old Testament times God did not really like the bloody sacrifices people offered to Him according to religious law. The God of Israel said, "I desire mercy, not sacrifice, and acknowledgment of God rather than burnt offerings." (Hos. 6:6). "'The multitude of your sacrifices—what are they to Me?' says the LORD. 'I have more than enough of burnt offerings, of rams and the fat of fattened animals; I have no pleasure in the blood of bulls and lambs and goats.'" (Isa. 1:11). By the time of Jesus, God wanted people to move beyond this primitive form of religion once and for all. It had served its purpose and its day was ended. A final, universal sacrifice—for all people for all time—got the job done and allowed humanity to progress to higher levels of spirituality, once they had the opportunity to hear about Christ.

I do not believe that people who are capable of atoning for their own sins and who need to do so to learn their lesson will benefit from a *literal* vicarious atonement by Jesus on the cross. But the concept of a substitutionary sacrifice in the person of the crucified Christ may be particularly useful and even literally real in cases where people are not responsible for their own sinful actions, such as young children, the mentally retarded, the senile, and the insane; as well as the sins of people who sinned so much that personal atonement would take far longer than is necessary for them to be reformed. In such cases, to use an Eastern expression, it could be said that Jesus chose to take on a lot of "bad karma" he didn't deserve, because of his great compassion.

In a more archetypal and mystical sense, I believe that the cross sums up for all humanity the travail of man receiving the penalty of sin, and in some sense is thus a collective atonement—because Christ on the Cross represented all mankind in the same way that Adam, the first man, did when he was expelled from the Garden. Paul called Jesus "the last Adam" (1 Cor. 15:45) and "the second man" (vs. 47), the culmination of the human condition and its collective restoration. As Paul put it, "For God was pleased to have all His fullness dwell in him, and through him to reconcile to Himself all things, whether things on earth or things in heaven, by making peace through his blood, shed on the cross." (Col. 1:20). Note that the power of the cross is to reconcile *all things*, not only to save people who believe in Christianity. John said that "if anybody does sin, we have one who speaks to the

Father in our defense—Jesus Christ, the Righteous One. He is the atoning sacrifice for our sins [Christians'], and not only for ours but also for the sins of the whole world." (1 John 2:1-2).

The True Meaning of the Cross—The Incarnation and Divine Nature

Beyond atonement, there are more significant ways of understanding the cross of Christ that do not depend on the traditions of any particular culture, nor restrict the love and mercy of God according to a technical, legalistic concept of justice. Furthermore, just because Jesus died a sacrificial death on the cross does not mean he died to allow us to escape from eternal torment. If condemnation to a never-ending hell is the penalty for sin, then why doesn't Jesus have to burn in hell forever if he died to pay the penalty for our sins? Logically, Jesus would be required to spend *eternity* in the lowest depth of hell, taking on the punishment of countless terrible sinners, if the doctrines of eternal hell and vicarious atonement are to be literally believed.

Much of the importance of the cross of Christ is in something other than its atoning function. Yes, Jesus died on the cross to enable us to be saved, but saved from what? Certainly not an endless hell. There is a deeper meaning to the sacrificial death of Jesus that does not include the hideous notion that God planned to burn billions of people alive for all eternity unless one man died a particular type of death. We can begin to understand the issue by recognizing Jesus' true nature as a human manifestation of the divine, what is usually called the *incarnation* of God. The Apostle Paul tells us that God had to become a human being in order to reach us where we are, to save us from human nature and help us rise into our higher spiritual nature as mature children of God. God came to earth in the form of Jesus for the same reason Jesus ate with sinners and tax collectors: because we need Him to become who God wants us to be, and we cannot reach Him unless He makes the first move. Forgiveness must come from the one who is offended; a helping hand must be extended by the one who has the power.

According to Paul, Jesus Christ, "being in very nature God, did not consider equality with God something to be grasped, but made himself nothing, taking the very nature of a servant, being made in human likeness. And being found in appearance as a man, he humbled himself and became obedient to death—even death on a cross!

Therefore God exalted him to the highest place and gave him the name that is above every name..." And here comes the part of this passage we have already seen in Part One: "… that at the name of Jesus every knee should bow, in heaven and on earth and under the earth, and every tongue confess that Jesus Christ is Lord, to the glory of God the Father." (Phil. 2:6-11). Now we can understand the context of Paul's point about universal reconciliation! It is made possible because of the incarnation of God in Christ, and the cruel death God experienced on the cross while in human form.

By manifesting Himself in the flesh as the perfect human being, Jesus of Nazareth, God's plan was to come to us sinners on earth and draw us to Himself in heaven. By dying on the cross, God could reach both the living and the dead by showing all people how much He loves us—so much that He is willing to go through a horrific torture and death to make His perfect love known and develop a relationship with us. We saw in Part One that Jesus said when he is "lifted up from the earth" he will "draw all men to himself" (John 12:32). Here's the next verse: "He said this to show the kind of death he was going to die." (vs. 33). Jesus was explaining to his disciples that by being lifted up on the cross, the whole world will be lifted up into salvation!

When we consider the cross of Christ, we should be struck by the fact that God is submitting to the worst aspects of human life: pain and death. The Bible tells us that pain and death are the bitter fruits of sin. Therefore, by taking on pain and death, God is taking on the penalty of sin. God does not sin, so He does not deserve this, but He chooses to endure the cross anyway, precisely because it is God's will to forgive us of our sins. By tasting of sin's penalty through Jesus Christ on the cross, God gains a whole new dimension of His nature and character. God can truly empathize with the anguish of human existence. Empathy is the beginning of mercy, and without mercy there can be no forgiveness. Because of the cross, God truly knows the human condition. He has lived it, in the person of Jesus Christ. God knows suffering and injustice. He knows the cruelty of evil. God can relate to man and his struggles in a much more intimate way, because He has been a man. Yes, God loves us *that much*—so much that He was willing to go through the cross to reach our hearts.

Believe it or not, God even knows what it's like to lose faith. Hanging on the cross, near death, Jesus cried out, "My God, my God, why have you forsaken me?" (Mat. 27:46). In his dying moments as a man, God Himself actually lost faith in God—paradoxical and mysterious though it may seem. As human beings naturally do, Jesus wondered, *How could God have allowed such a terrible thing to happen to me? What is the purpose of this suffering? Doesn't God love me?* Jesus' full humanity does not detract from his divinity. In fact, it only enhances it, for it adds an important aspect to the Christian God that is unique among all religious faiths. God loves us so much, He was even willing to endure the ultimate torment of despair, showing us there is nothing He wouldn't do to help us love Him.

This is why the cross was necessary for our salvation. We can look to the cross and see that God understands and has experienced human misery to the utmost degree—both physical and psychological struggles—which enables God to forgive us for all our weaknesses and any wrong thing we might think or do as a result of the human condition. Knowing the extraordinary level of God's compassion towards us—even those of us who suffer to the point of despair—we can love God as our Father, not merely as a stern Lord who judges us strictly according to our sins when we die. Because of the cross, we know that God is in the business of understanding and forgiveness, not tyranny and wrath.

Indeed, it is because of Jesus' sacrificial death that we can truly love God. Without it, we could only fear God and tremble in anticipation of punishment for our inherent sinfulness, which we cannot control no matter how hard we try to avoid committing sins. The crucifixion saves us from our own fear and guilt in the face of an angry god of our imagination. This is hell indeed, a fire hotter than any lurid description of fundamentalist preachers and tracts. By understanding the amazing act of compassion that God demonstrated on the cross, we can escape this hellish spiritual condition and find the kingdom of heaven within our hearts, in the form of a mature, authentic love for a God who truly loves us. We can know, as Paul taught, "that God was reconciling the world to Himself in Christ, not counting men's sins against them." (2 Cor. 5:19).

The True Meaning of the Cross—The Significance of the Resurrection

According to the testimony of eye-witnesses recorded in the Bible, Jesus Christ rose from the dead. After being tortured and killed, he was buried in a tomb, but on the third day the tomb was found empty and Jesus was seen alive and restored to glory. Not only was he restored, but his glory and power were even greater than before! The resurrection was the culmination of God's plan to prove His love for all people. If Jesus had not conquered death and shown this publicly, he would have gone down in history as just another radical Jewish false prophet who was executed by the Romans for treason. We never would have known he was the divine being he claimed to be, and we never would have understood God's absolute power to change evil into good.

When Isaiah wrote his moving prophecy about the suffering Messiah, emphasizing that at the time of his appearance "we esteemed him not," that "we considered him stricken by God" because he "carried our sorrows" (Isa. 53:3-4), this great Hebrew prophet was accurately foretelling the way people viewed Jesus Christ when he went to the cross. In the time and culture of Jesus, being crucified was the ultimate insult to a man's character. The Old Testament says that people who are hung on a tree are accursed (Deut. 21:23), and this was interpreted by first-century Jews to include death by crucifixion. For both the Jews and the Romans, this form of execution was reserved for the most heinous criminals and was the sign of a person considered by society to be totally worthless—worthy only of a humiliating torture, a long, lingering death of excruciating pain, hanging naked on a post for the public to gawk at and ridicule. Jesus was forced to wear a crown of thorns, was spat upon, and was even made to carry his own cross to the place of execution, all while crowds of spectators hurled insults at him. After Jesus was sentenced to death, his small band of disciples dispersed rather than acclaiming him as their leader. Even Peter, the "rock" on which Jesus would build his church, denied Jesus three times. Nobody wanted anything to do with a crucified man.

The fact that God picked such an unlikely man for His own incarnation shows that no one is ever accursed, rejected, or damned by God. Not even a person that all of society regards with contempt is actually condemned by anything other than human arrogance and hatred. Even those who are considered to be the worst criminals and social outcasts are loved by their Maker, and can always still be saved. Jesus was considered a blasphemer, a traitor, a dangerous cult leader and a charlatan. He was believed by many to be possessed by demons. People didn't love him, but God loved him. God chose a vessel of dishonor to fill to the brim with His Holy Spirit—and He did this to prove us wrong about our limited, fearful, self-serving conceptions of the divine. When Jesus was resurrected, the judgments of the world were proven wrong, and God was proven right. A man who died a death of ultimate dishonor, who most people thought would go to hell, instead became the only man in human history to rise in glory from the grave.

Whenever we look at the weak and the downtrodden, the sick and the ugly, the crazy and the criminal among us, we are to realize that they too are loved by God, and that they too will one day meet us in heaven. We are all sinners, all imperfect—and we are commanded by God not to judge one another, but to love one another as brothers and sisters, all children of our heavenly Father. "A new command I give you: Love one another. As I have loved you, so you must love one another." (John 13:34). There are no exceptions, no people unworthy of our love and God's love. As Jesus said, "I tell you the truth, whatever you did for one of the least of these brothers of mine, you did for me." (Mat. 25:40).

The cross of Christ is a symbol of hope for all people, that God loves every one of us and will not abandon us even when we lose faith and abandon Him. Even the most hopeless souls—even the unbelieving and sinful dead—have hope in the saving power of Jesus Christ. God wants us to know that He loves us with a deep and abiding love, no matter who we are and what we have done, no matter whether people embrace us or condemn us, no matter whether we are in the flesh or in the spirit. God's love is infinite and can overcome all obstacles. The cross of Christ is God's way of proving the unfathomable depth and invincible power of His love for us—for *all* of us—so that we can know for sure that God's love can never fail. There is no limit on what God will do for us when we need His grace. There is nowhere God will not go, nothing God will not do, to help people find peace and forgiveness and return to Him in heaven.

The incarnation of God into the body of a crucified man, and his miraculous resurrection from the dead, prove that nothing is impossible and that God will do whatever it takes to see us saved. Before it happened, who would have thought it possible? So if you think universal salvation is impossible for God, think again. God never gives up on anyone; He has a plan to make all things right. That's the whole point of the cross. It has nothing to do with saving people from an endless torture in hell.

Exclusionary Teachings—The "Narrow Gate" and the Rich Man

Now that we have discussed one of the most central themes of the Christian Gospel and disposed of its faulty yet common interpretation, let's move on to some simpler issues that are raised by believers in eternal hell. These are simple because they seem to be quite straightforward when one reads the Bible with a predetermined viewpoint that salvation is exclusive rather than inclusive of all people. Indeed, some Bible passages do seem to suggest an exclusive heaven, which can imply that some people will forever be shut out and left in hell—if these teachings are read out of context or without a proper understanding of the overall message of the Bible about God's plan of ultimate reconciliation.

One of these questions that is raised in objection to universalism is this: *What about the "narrow gate" to heaven?* Jesus teaches that the way to heaven is difficult and most people will not make it in. He tells us to "Enter through the narrow gate. For wide is the gate and broad is the road that leads to destruction, and many enter through it. But small is the gate and narrow the road that leads to life, and only a few find it." (Mat. 7:13-14). Does this mean that only a few people will enter heaven but the majority of people will never find it, having taken the broad road to eternal hell? At first glance, that might seem to be what Jesus was saying.

Nevertheless, we must realize that Jesus does not say the people who don't find the narrow gate to heaven will *forever* be left out. That is an assumption made by Christians who believe in eternal hell. If they understood the correct meaning of the word *aionios* used in the Greek New Testament to describe what Jesus said was the duration of hell, they would realize that Jesus cannot have meant that the gates of heaven are forever closed to the residents of hell. It is only for a period of time—perhaps a long one, but only an age in the infinity of eternity—that some people will be in "Gehenna" or the "Lake of Fire" rather than in the heavenly Kingdom.

This alternative view is confirmed by examining the original Greek text of Mat. 7:14 about the narrow gate. The word "find" was written in a tense that would more accurately be translated as "finding."

Jesus was saying that few people were finding the gate to heaven *at that time*, because few were responding to his teachings that lead to salvation. "Few are those finding it," says Jesus according to Young's Literal Translation—as well as several other versions of the Bible that strive for maximum accuracy. Jesus was not making a prediction that only a few will ever find salvation in the future, as the more common English translations imply. Just a minor misunderstanding of Greek verb tenses can change the whole tone and implication of an important statement by the Lord.

Let's take a closer look at this issue of the narrow gate and put it into context. Jesus told a story about how hard it is for a rich man to get to heaven. Burdened by materialism and greed like a camel carrying a heavy load, the wealthy may not be able to fit through the "narrow gate" to heaven, because their inflated ego and focus on worldly things prevents them from moving forward spiritually. A camel would have to pass through a small opening naked, stripped of any material goods that could cause it to get stuck; and similarly, a rich man seeking the true paradise would have to give up the craving for money rather than clinging to it, because, as the saying goes, "you can't take it with you." Jesus said to his disciples, "I tell you the truth, it is hard for a rich man to enter the kingdom of heaven. Again I tell you, it is easier for a camel to go through the eye of a needle than for a rich man to enter the kingdom of God." (Mat. 19:23-24).

There is also a double meaning here, in that a literal eye of a needle is tiny and a camel obviously could never fit through it unless the laws of physics were suspended. Does that mean the rich are condemned to hell? From what Jesus said, it sure sounds like it, and that was the reaction of the disciples, too. Like many Christians who assume that sinners can never pass through the narrow gate to heaven, they assumed it is impossible for the rich to be saved just like it is impossible for a camel to pass through the eye of a needle: "When the disciples heard this, they were greatly astonished and asked, 'Who then can be saved?'" (vs. 25). Jesus answered by challenging their assumption: "Jesus looked at them and said, 'With man this is impossible, but with God all things are possible.'" (vs. 26). What Jesus was saying is that even if it's very, very difficult for someone to get to heaven, *God will find a way* to make it happen. God will make the seemingly impossible, possible!

So even if most people do take the broad road to destruction, that doesn't mean they cannot someday still find their way back to the straight and narrow path that leads to the gate to heaven. It is a natural human tendency to assume that death spells the end of our choices and our chance to grow and change. If a life was lived in sin and unbelief, we find it hard to imagine that something could change for the better in the afterlife—just like we cannot imagine a camel passing through the eye of a needle. But Jesus assures us that God has the power to make miracles a reality. If we doubt this, Jesus' own miraculous life and resurrection from the dead is all the proof we need.

A related question concerns a parable told by Jesus that has similar themes of exclusion from heaven and the likelihood of selfish rich people going to hell: *What about the Rich Man and Lazarus?* In this story, a rich man who lived in the lap of luxury dies and finds himself tormented in the fires of hell, while a poor man who begged and ate scraps at his door goes to paradise when he dies and is together with the great patriarch Abraham. The point of the story is to warn the rich that they must have compassion and give liberally to the poor if they hope to attain the aionian life and blessings of righteousness, whereas if they indulge in their wealth and forget those who have little, they will receive the aionian chastisement. In a more metaphorical sense, this may also be a parable prophesying the redemption of the Gentiles (Lazarus) who had received little from God, and the judgment and suffering of the Jews (the Rich Man) who had received much of God's favor until the time of Christ but did not appreciate the blessings they were given. In general, it is one of many stories told by Jesus that feature the theme of reversal of fortune brought about by divine justice, the "last becoming first" and the "first becoming last."

The reason fundamentalist Christians point to the story of the Rich Man and Lazarus as evidence of eternal hell is because of this passage describing the plight of the Rich Man: "In hell [Hades], where he was in torment, he looked up and saw Abraham far away, with Lazarus by his side. So he called to him, 'Father Abraham, have pity on me and send Lazarus to dip the tip of his finger in water and cool my tongue, because I am in agony in this fire.' But Abraham replied, 'Son, remember that in your lifetime you received your good things, while Lazarus received bad things, but now he is comforted here and you are in agony. And besides all this, between us and you a great chasm has been fixed, so that those who want to go from here to you cannot, nor can anyone cross over from there to us.'" (Luke 16:23-26). This statement about a "great chasm" that is "fixed" to prevent the Rich Man from crossing over from hell to heaven seems to support the idea that some people may have to spend eternity in the torments of hell.

However, that is not a reasonable interpretation. It may be that Jesus was simply trying to impress upon his audience that if a person is wicked enough to go to a place of suffering after death, they will have to serve their term in this hellish place with no relief until justice is done. Jesus told another parable about a wicked servant who owed a huge debt to his master, the king. He couldn't pay, so he begged the king to forgive his debts, and the king decided to have mercy on him. But after that, the wicked servant went to one of his fellows and demanded that he pay him a debt he owed him, and when he could not pay, he decided *not* to be merciful as the king had been to him: he had his fellow servant thrown into debtor's prison. When word of this cruel and hypocritical deed got around, "In anger his master turned him over to the jailers to be tortured, until he should pay back all he owed." Jesus adds that "This is how my heavenly Father will treat each of you unless you forgive your brother from your heart." (Mat. 18:34-35). The point is, if we live a merciless and selfish life we will find ourselves tormented in the prison of hell after we die—but only until we pay off our debt, that is, settle our accounts with God and those we wronged. This parable upholds the reality of divine judgment and hell, but directly contradicts the claim that hell is eternal.

The story of the Rich Man and Lazarus uses strong, vivid language, but it is the language of parable and metaphor. The agony of the fire and the Rich Man's thirst are not literal, though they are very real. The "great chasm" preventing him from crossing from hell to heaven does not imply that he must remain in hell forever, but simply emphasizes the point that once we find ourselves in hell, we will have to endure the full judgment of God ordained for us until justice is served.

I believe what Jesus is teaching in stories about a narrow gate to heaven and a rich man who goes to hell is simply that many souls are not ready yet to receive the blessings of paradise, but must first face fiery judgments to purge them of selfish desires and other forms of sin. Jesus is warning people that if they do not try as hard as possible to follow the path of the Spirit during their life, there will be unpleasant consequences after death. People who refuse to walk in the way of God, choosing for themselves a life of materialistic riches, gluttonous pleasure, and self-absorption, rather than faithfulness to the Lord and selfless service to their fellow man, will indeed find themselves on the outside of heaven looking in after they die. Their ego will be deflated and destroyed. They will feel the burning fires of regret and loss within their consciousness, knowing that they wasted a chance on earth to strive to grow closer to God and to live in a godly way. They will have to endure difficult lessons prepared for them by God to help their soul rise above the things of the flesh which they had so enthusiastically embraced in their disdain for the things of the Spirit.

God prefers that we voluntarily choose to turn away from corruption and evil, and start walking the path that leads directly to heaven. But if we fail to make this choice during our lifetime, then God will find it necessary to teach us through the consequences of a more painful path we have chosen, which temporarily leads away from heaven and into a hellish state. For those who take the broad road to destruction, they will face the firm discipline of God, their Father, who will see that they learn their lessons the hard way—so that they, too, will one day take their place in the heavenly Kingdom with Jesus, alongside Abraham and all the prophets and the saints.

Exclusionary Teachings—The "Only Way" and Non-Christians

There are a few other well-known Bible passages that seem to promote an exclusionary view of heaven, and by inference in the minds of fundamentalists, an eternal hell for those who don't make it in. The most noteworthy one we have not yet covered is Jesus' assertion that he is the "only way." This is typically interpreted by conservative Christians to mean that if a person does not follow the Christian religion, one cannot be saved and is therefore lost forever.

Here is what Jesus actually said: "I am the way and the truth and the life. No one comes to the Father except through me. If you really knew me, you would know my Father as well. From now on, you do know Him and have seen Him." (John 14:6-7). Jesus was talking to his disciples about his divine nature. He was explaining that if anyone wants to know what God is like, they should look at Jesus, because Jesus is God in human form. That means the character of Jesus is the same as God's character—His love, mercy, forgiveness, desire for righteousness and justice and the salvation of all people.

We know that the way of life Jesus lived was all about reaching out to the poor, the suffering and the downtrodden. He often made a point of criticizing arrogant religious leaders who thought only they were saved and nobody else was good enough to receive God's favor. For example, Jesus scolded the Pharisees for their fanatical and misguided religiosity, saying, "Woe to you, teachers of the law and Pharisees, you hypocrites! You shut the kingdom of heaven in men's faces. You yourselves do not enter, nor will you let those enter who are trying to. … You travel over land and sea to win a single convert, and when he becomes one, you make him twice as much a son of hell [Gehenna] as you are." (Mat. 23:13,15). Jesus also went into the temple and overturned the money-changers' tables in disgust, because they had turned religion into a commercial enterprise and a pompous show, sucking the spirituality out of it in the name of tradition and legalism.

See any similarities to today's fundamentalists? Jesus would be just as upset with them today for some of the things they believe and do as he was with the Pharisees and Jewish temple leaders of his own time and culture. The common thread tying them together is their *exclusionary* attitude. "Better believe and do things just the way we do, or you'll be shut out of God's Kingdom forever!"—that's the kind of religion Jesus opposed.

When Jesus said that no one comes to the Father except through him, he was saying that if people want to learn about God, they should learn about Jesus. That was especially true for the people living in first-century Israel who actually had the opportunity to meet Jesus personally this side of the grave. For them, in the midst of their corrupt society full of religious hypocrites and imperial brutality, it probably was literally true that following Jesus was the only way people could really develop a relationship with God *as Father*, rather than as some tyrant of the Jewish or Roman imagination. When Jesus spoke of God as "Father," the word he used in Aramaic, the language he spoke, was *Abba*, a term of endearment similar to the English word "Daddy." What a revolutionary concept, that ordinary people can pray to God and develop a close relationship with Him on such friendly and intimate terms! For us today, it remains true that to know Jesus is to know God in a way we cannot know Him otherwise, and we would do well to look to the example of Jesus for evidence of the way God works and who He really is. But that does not mean people are condemned to eternal hell if they don't follow the Christian religion. Would your daddy abandon you in a pit of fire? *Some daddy indeed!*

As a final note on this topic, when Jesus said he is the way, the truth, and the life, that indicates that to come to the Father through Jesus Christ means something other than to profess a particular religious creed. What it means is that coming to know the Father is a process of following the way of Jesus, living a Christlike life, recognizing the truth of who God really is and who we really are as children of God, and our responsibility to live accordingly. It has little or nothing to do with the details of our religious beliefs, what church we attend or don't attend, or anything else that fundamentalist Christians so often like to emphasize. A person needs to follow in the *spirit* of Jesus rather than necessarily believe certain theological doctrines about him. I believe if people in another religious tradition outside of Christianity live according to the teachings of Jesus but do not believe he is God or the Messiah, they can still be saved because they are following the way taught by Jesus, which is the way of spiritual rebirth. There have been many saintly men and women who were not "Christians"—but who in Jesus' eyes may actually have been more Christian than most who call themselves by that name.

But what about this problem: *Didn't Jesus say people who don't believe in him are condemned?* "Whoever believes in him is not condemned, but whoever does not believe stands condemned already because he has not believed in the name of God's one and only Son." (John 3:18). That's Jesus talking. Doesn't sound too good for non-Christians—but let's read on to get some context. Jesus continues: "This is the verdict: Light has come into the world, but men loved darkness instead of light because their deeds were evil. Everyone who does evil hates the light, and will not come into the light for fear that his deeds will be exposed. But whoever lives by the truth comes into the light, so that it may be seen plainly that what he has done has been done through God." (vss. 19-20).

Problem solved. The point Jesus was making is not that anyone throughout history is condemned to hell unless they believe in Christ. His point—which was addressed to the people of his own time who knew him—was that many who had the opportunity to meet the Messiah and see that he was full of divine light did not recognize him and live by his truth and light, because they were already evil and did evil deeds. Their wicked character caused them to fail to perceive God's light or fail to follow His truth which would expose their wickedness. It is *not* that people are evil and condemned *because* they don't believe in Christ; it's the opposite. Fundamentalists have it backwards, arguing that salvation comes from a profession of doctrinal belief, so they completely mis-interpret the point of Jesus' statement about condemnation for those who refused to recognize and follow him when he came to them. Jesus was observing that belief and action—whether right or wrong, good or evil—flow naturally from the quality of one's character.

Exclusionary Teachings—"Born Again" Christians and Unsaved Fanatics

Another often misunderstood issue is what Jesus said about spiri-tual rebirth. Fundamentalists, who like to consider themselves "born-again Christians," ask: *What about the need to be born again to see heav-en?* The idea is that people who are not born again in the Holy Spirit are going to hell—and presumably that is most people, even some who are Christians but "don't make the cut" in God's exclusive club.

What Jesus actually said is this: "I tell you the truth, no one can see the kingdom of God unless he is born again. … [N]o one can enter the kingdom of God unless he is born of water and the Spirit." (John 3:3,5). Many Christians interpret "born of water" to mean baptism into the Christian religion, and "born of Spirit" to mean a second conversion experience including special gifts such as speaking in unknown tongues (*glossolalia*, a form of ecstatic speech), miraculous healings or other events signifying the supernatural power of God's Spirit coming into one's life. They argue that if a person has not undergone these two mile-stones of Christian faith, one has not escaped the fate of eternal hell.

In both cases this is merely an interpretation, and does not neces-sarily follow from what Jesus said. Jesus was talking to a thick-headed Jewish religious leader, Nicodemus, who had great difficulty grasp-ing anything beyond literal and worldly notions. Jesus was trying to open Nicodemus' mind to the value of letting God move him in new spiritual directions. He likened the Holy Spirit to a "wind" that "blows wherever it pleases" (vs. 8), in contrast to the limitations of the fleshly life and a literalistic, legalistic, carnally oriented mindset.

I believe what Jesus really meant is that everyone is born in the physical sense, from the water of the womb, but only some have experienced the spiritual rebirth that comes from developing an authentic relationship with God. Until we do this, we cannot see heaven, either in this life or the next. Being born again in the Spirit might indeed include amazing or even supernatural occurrences, but it is not necessarily a formulaic display that a Pentecostal church would applaud as evidence of God's presence. More likely, it could be a gradual transformation of one's character and life, replacing the fleshly and worldly focus with a truly spiritual and otherworldly holiness and maturity of being. It is about discovering one's true nature and limitless potential as a child of God, created in His image, and growing up into the station of a mature son or daughter serving the Father in heaven, while yet living on earth. Being born again means being made new in the image of Christ, putting aside the fallen ego that is destined to die and replacing it with the living Spirit of the divine that can abide eternally within us.

So if we don't need to be a stereotypical "born-again Christian" to avoid eternal hell, *What about the people that Jesus says he will send away, saying "I never knew you"?* This question is in reference to the following warning of Jesus: "Not everyone who says to me, 'Lord, Lord,' will enter the kingdom of heaven, but only he who does the will of my Father who is in heaven. Many will say to me on that day, 'Lord, Lord, did we not prophesy in your name, and in your name drive out demons and perform many miracles?' Then I will tell them plainly, 'I never knew you. Away from me, you evildoers!'" (Mat. 7:21-23).

Fundamentalist Christians use this passage as evidence that some people who call themselves Christian will nevertheless be damned to hell. They take this as an argument for a very limited, exclusive salvation available only to the very best, most ultra-religious Christians. In reality, these "ultra-Christian" folks are the ones who should be worried! The people Jesus is talking about sound like fundamentalist preachers—but for some reason Jesus says he never knew them. What could possibly keep sincere Christians from knowing Jesus Christ, despite being so fervent in their Christianity that they are prophesying, performing exorcisms and miracles in Jesus' name? Could it be that they have created a false image of Jesus in their minds, and therefore they cannot see the real Jesus Christ in their hearts? Could it be that, blinded by fear and fierce religiosity, their vision of God is actually evil?

Jesus warned his followers about hard-hearted Christians who will preach false doctrines, and he said we can know them by the fruits of their teachings. "Watch out for false prophets. They come to you in sheep's clothing, but inwardly they are ferocious wolves. By their fruit you will recognize them. Do people pick grapes from thornbushes, or figs from thistles? Likewise every good tree bears good fruit, but a bad tree bears bad fruit." (Mat. 7:15-17). Many Christians go around telling people they are going to burn in hell forever unless they convert to the Christian religion. They may seem like true believers, holy and pure. But the fruit of this kind of religion is most often rotten and foul. The traditional doctrine of hell is a bitter and poisonous fruit, and it has left a dark stain on Christianity. Hell on people's lips has led to hell on earth in the form of insanity, hatred and intolerance, heresy trials, torture chambers, burnings at the stake, religious wars, brutal colonialism, fanatical sects, broken homes, and many people losing their faith.

So if anyone needs to watch out that when they die and meet Jesus he might tell them "I never knew you," it is probably the fundamentalist fanatics who are so quick to consign large portions of humanity to their imaginary god's sadistic dungeon. Even so, "knew" is past tense. Jesus didn't say he "never would" know them. Fundamentalists just haven't known Jesus *yet* for who he really is: God's ambassador of love to all humanity.

To conclude this discussion about Bible passages that seem to suggest an exclusive heaven restricted to God's "elect" rather than salvation for all people, I believe Jesus emphasized the difficulty of attaining heaven because he wanted to push people to their spiritual limit. His aim was to challenge souls to rise to heights they never before imagined they could achieve. So he talked about a narrow gate, the danger of living for selfish and materialistic ends, the importance of inviting the Holy Spirit into one's life and following the way shown by Christ, and the striking fact that some people will die and think they are going straight to paradise but instead will be told by their Lord that they fell far short of the goal. The meaning of these stories is not to terrorize people with a threat of eternal rejection by their Maker and a never-ending torture after death; it is simply a warning that we must try our hardest if we truly seek to walk the path of Christ and become worthy of standing beside him in the Kingdom.

No Hell? Party On, Dude!

Now that we have dealt with some of the Biblical issues, let's turn our attention to some more philosophical and practical issues that are raised by people who doubt the teaching of universal reconciliation. Probably the most commonly asked question is, *Why should we avoid sin if everyone is saved?* Many people seem to think that if God saves everyone in the end, then we might as well sin as much as we want right now. This is used as an objection to Christian Universalism, an attempt to show that there must be an eternal hell or else people would never live a Christian life.

There are two main problems with this viewpoint. First of all, Christian Universalists don't believe there is no such thing as hell. There definitely is divine punishment for anyone who needs it, as much as they need it. As we have already seen, there are many verses in the Bible where Jesus and other prophets and teachers speak of some kind of chastisement of the wicked. In case there is any doubt about sound Biblical teaching on this issue, let this explicit warning of Paul drive home the point: "Do not be deceived: God cannot be mocked. A man reaps what he sows. The one who sows to please his sinful nature, from that nature will reap destruction; the one who sows to please the Spirit, from the Spirit will reap [age-lasting] life." (Gal. 6:7-8).

What Christian Universalists believe is that hell is temporary, a *re-formative* punishment rather than vindictive and eternal. It is a question of the purpose of hell, not the existence of hell. Is hell a place where God condemns people who didn't measure up to His standards, and forces them to endure horrific tortures forever and ever as a way to get revenge against them for failing to be or do what He wanted? Or, on the other hand, is hell a way that God purifies us of our imperfections, destroying the sinful nature within us to set us straight, putting us through some necessary corrective experiences such that we may understand our failings and can improve ourselves and be made ready to enter heaven? Christian Universalists would say the latter is the true hell, and the other view is just a perverted fantasy about a sadistic god. Nobody wants to go through any type of hell, but hell is real for unrepentant sinners; it's just not a permanent state of being.

Let's explore the issue further, so that it will be crystal clear why hell need not be eternal to serve as an effective deterrent against sin. If you choose not to go out and commit crimes and break the law because you fear the police, courts and prison, then it is clear that you shouldn't go out and sin against God and your fellow man even though hell is not eternal. A prison term is not eternal torment either, but it is enough to prevent most people from doing a crime and having to serve time. In other words, punishment does not have to be infinite in duration or intensity to deter people from doing bad deeds.

I think all reasonable people can agree that punishments should always fit the crime and be justly measured out, rather than grossly exceeding what is just. For God to throw somebody into an eternal fire with no hope of ever gaining release, just because they committed sins during one short mortal life, would be unjust since the punishment would not fit the crime. If punishment is just, people will fear it and refrain from doing things that incur punishment; but if it is unjustly excessive, people will be no more likely to avoid such actions, but would definitely be filled with more anger and hate for the system and the One who created it. If God wants us to love Him, as the Bible says He does, then He cannot be unjust in punishing, since it is impossible for human beings to truly love one who is unjust, whether another human or any other being.

Secondly, I believe God wants us to avoid sin and act in a righteous manner not because of fear of punishment in the afterlife, but because of our love for God and for what is good, in and of itself. All animals have a natural, biological instinct to avoid pain. If humans are only refraining from sin and doing good deeds because they fear being burned alive in hell for eternity, that does not make us any better than the beasts.

We are called to develop our spiritual faculties, the most important of which is love: love for God, love for our fellow man, and love for what is good, right, and true. In order to grow spiritually and become more like Christ, the example we are trying to follow, we must learn to love rather than fear—and we must learn how to *act* out of love rather than fear. Jesus Christ didn't start a ministry to feed the poor, show compassion to the lost and lonely, forgive people of their sins and encourage people to rise to a higher spiritual potential because he was afraid that his Father would burn him with fire if he didn't do so. Certainly not! The fear of endless hellfire was not even in Jesus' mind! He lived the way he did because he wanted to do good, and it was in his nature to love other people and to show them the right way to live through his wonderful example. If we want to call ourselves "Christian," we must strive to be more like Christ, and that means putting aside a fear-based motivation for our actions and lifestyle and instead attempting to live rightly because we love God and we love other people—not because we are afraid that if we sin too much or we don't perform enough good deeds, God will torture us forever in hell.

Some Like It Hot: "Choosing" Eternal Hell?

There is a popular theory that some people simply don't have any interest in going to heaven; they actually prefer not to have a relationship with God, and if that means eternal hell, then so be it. *Don't souls have free will to reject God and choose to stay in hell forever?* This idea probably arises from simple observation of the fact that some people choose to stay away from church, don't pray, don't live a Christian lifestyle, and may even immerse themselves in the "things of Satan": drugs, alcoholism, sexual promiscuity and perversions, and all manner of notorious sins. The theory goes that if a person is like this now, on earth, they will remain that way for eternity unless they change before they die. Therefore, eternal hell is a matter of personal choice, not a decision by God to condemn anyone. Because God respects our free will, He will allow us to choose hell if that is our desire.

Boy, doesn't that get God off the hook! People like the free will theory of hell because they don't have to think of God as a monster who holds people in the fire while they scream in agony for forgiveness, begging to have another chance that will never be given. If some souls are innately stubborn and evil, preferring the devil's domain despite its trouble and pain rather than the sublime and holy abode of God, then we can write them off and stop worrying about them—they've got what they want. But the problem with the idea that some people "choose" eternal hell is that upon closer examination, it proves to be absurd.

For one thing, why would God create a soul that would never seek Him? It is certainly true that some souls will not develop a relationship with God while on earth, because they are deluded and seduced by the things of the flesh. But after physical death, the human spirit is liberated from these things that may hold us back from higher spiritual realities. It is not possible for a soul to resist God forever, for one simple reason: God has created us with a nature to seek the divine and to learn from our mistakes. If God had done otherwise, it would be sheer cruelty. Imagine a parent deliberately choosing to create a child that would *always* rebel, *never* grow up, and be *intrinsically unable* to feel love for the source of its being. The child was created to be forever trapped in an endless, meaningless cycle of rebellion and punishment, never learning, never changing, always hating. This is unthinkable! Surely God is better than to create people to be this way. If they are, it is only a temporary condition inspired by the conditions of their life. Seeking God and progressing toward a higher goal is ingrained in our very nature, and this is especially evident when the spirit is separated from the animalistic flesh and the limitations, desires and motivations that come with life in a physical body.

The Bible tells us that we were made in God's own image and likeness (see Gen. 1:26-27). This godly part of our being is incompatible with hatred for God and the things of the divine. Human beings are certainly granted some degree of free will, but not to the degree that many of us tend to think. On earth, we are free to seek the things of the flesh rather than the spirit, because this life is a test for our spiritual development. We are free even to deny our own innermost nature—the nature of God within us—and to act as though we are mere animals, full of carnal cravings, selfishness and violence, and lacking a higher meaning for our existence beyond the things of this world. But much of this freedom is illusory, and will perish along with the fleshly ego when we die. In God's world beyond, we will remember who we really are and face the consequences of the misuse and misunderstanding of our freedom. The judgments of God will restore us to our true spiritual selves, children of our heavenly Father.

True, some people *in this life* have much less spirituality than others and more focus on materialism, but I believe that will eventually even out in the afterlife. Some people are burdened with a more rebellious flesh than others here on earth, due to genetic tendencies and the mysteries of God's plan for each individual. Different souls may also have different personality traits which can only be changed through experiences that mold and shape the personality in new directions, either in this life or the next. The spirit of each person may also be relatively weaker or stronger, at a different stage of development than others, due to experiences prior to this life.

The bottom line is that I do not believe God would ever create a soul with the intrinsic desire to be damned. That would be incompatible with love and justice. Therefore, all souls desire to be saved, whether or not they realize what this means or why they should want it at this time. If we desire something, we will inevitably seek it—at least eventually we will, under the right conditions. Souls that do not seek salvation in this earthly life simply are too much under the influence of the desires of the flesh; but when the flesh falls away at death and the spirit is liberated, one will be returned to one's natural preponderance of inclinations, which on balance is to seek God. Therefore, in the afterlife all souls will desire to be redeemed, and will be willing to do whatever is necessary to be reconciled and reunited with their Creator.

In other words, human free will is not absolute, since God has programmed us all with a will to return to Him in the end. God "wants all men to be saved and to come to a knowledge of the truth. For there is one God and one mediator between God and men, the man Christ Jesus, who gave himself as a ransom for all men..." (1 Tim. 2:4-6). God gets what He wants, and He has a plan to make it happen—for *everyone*. Lest we believe God's desire for the salvation of all people is merely an empty wish, and God might be disappointed because rebellious humans will forever thwart His plans, God says, "so is My word that goes out from My mouth: It will not return to Me empty, but will accomplish what I desire and achieve the purpose for which I sent it." (Isa. 55:11). "My purpose will stand, and I will do all that I please... What I have said, that will I bring about; what I have planned, that will

I do." (46:10-11). God's will is supreme. Since God has said it doesn't please Him for some people to spend eternity unsaved, He simply will not allow that to happen. Our own puny free will cannot forever stand in the way of God's overarching plan of universal salvation.

To Hell and Back: Visions and Testimonies of the Netherworld

Some people believe that not everyone is saved because they have heard stories of people who claim to have gone to hell or were shown a vision of its terrible reality. They ask, *What about mystical and near-death experiences of hell?* Aren't these supernatural encounters proof that there really is a place of never-ending torment in the afterlife where some people are condemned?

Visions and mystical experiences of heaven or hell are a dime a dozen. Throughout history, numerous people have claimed to possess special insight about the afterlife, and the stories they tell often contradict each other in major ways. For every vision of a stereotypical hell of eternal torture, there are visions of a heaven where all people are included. For every vision of a stern and judgmental God, there are visions of a God who radiates unconditional love. Basing our theology and beliefs about the afterlife primarily on visionary experiences that people claim to have had is not a good idea, because we have no way of knowing who is credible and who is a liar, or which experiences are truly supernatural and which ones were the product of an overactive imagination, a vivid dream life, or a drug-induced hallucination.

That's not to say that some people have not really been to hell and back. The phenomenon of near-death experiences (NDEs), in which a person's spirit seemingly leaves the body and hovers over it, then journeys to other dimensions while the body and brain are clinically dead, is well documented, and some of these purported experiences are probably real. Only a small minority of NDE reports are of the hellish variety. In most cases, people say they went to a place of light and peace rather than darkness and suffering.

The few cases where people go to hell and return to tell the tale actually support the idea that God lets people out of hell rather than keeping them there eternally. Most NDE testimonies that include a trip to hell also include God responding to the lost soul's prayers, upon which the negative experience generally transforms into a positive one. Stories like these show that hell is not eternal, since people who go there are given the opportunity to escape, and do in fact leave when they are ready for repentance and God is ready to release them. Why else would the dead man on the operating table suddenly, miraculously come back to life and return with a story of going to hell, if not because God was merciful and allowed him another chance?

There are two things that the vast majority of near-death experiences seem to teach people about God and the afterlife: first, that there is a God who loves us more than we could even imagine; and second, that judgment and hell are real but not eternal. Most people who have an NDE come back as believers in a benevolent Higher Power and life after death, and embrace the teaching of universal salvation—specifically, a concept of restorative universalism, that the soul must only go through divine judgment as a way to learn spiritual lessons and be purged of evil in order to enter heaven. Very few NDEs convince people that there is such a thing as eternal damnation. In fact, eternal damnation is probably the number one traditional Christian doctrine that people *reject* after having such an experience. Dr. Ken Vincent, professor emeritus of psychology and an expert on the NDE phenomenon, writes that "Of all the theological explanations for the near-death experience (NDE), the Doctrine of Universal Salvation, also known as Universalism, is the most compatible with contemporary NDE accounts. ... Christian Universalism, a doctrine with solid support in the New Testament, blends seamlessly with the experience of NDErs."[6]

One feature of many near-death experiences is that the visions people see of the afterlife tend to correlate with their own expectations or beliefs, and are designed to challenge them in some way in their life using imagery that would be strongly motivating to that particular individual. In other words, NDEs seem to be tailored to each person's spiritual understanding and needs, rather than a uniform presentation of absolute truth. This suggests that some NDE visions of hell could be primarily designed to frighten people into changing their lifestyle—to stop sinning and become more righteous in their behavior. Perhaps some people can only be moved to change their ways by seeing horrible visions of hell, and that is why God allows the experience. We

---

[6] Vincent, Ken R. "The Near-Death Experience and Christian Universalism." *Journal of Near-Death Studies*, 22 (1), Fall 2003: 57-71. Republished online at http://www.near-death.com/experiences/origen021.html

cannot draw general theological conclusions from them. And the fact is, people with a strong belief in hell and judgment are more likely to have a NDE involving hellish imagery, which may indicate that some of these experiences are the product of a dying brain rather than a true supernatural vision of the afterlife.

Annihilationism: The Halfway Solution

When leaving one belief system and considering another, many people like to go halfway. Perhaps that's why in recent years, the idea of annihilation of the wicked has been gaining ground among conservative Christians who are uncomfortable with the traditional doctrine of eternal conscious torment. If God only *destroys* the unsaved—a final death penalty—rather than keeping them alive to suffer forever in hell with no hope of release, perhaps that's something we can live with. It's not nearly as bad as believing in a God who maintains an everlasting cosmic torture chamber. So let's consider it: *What about the possibility of annihilation of the wicked?*

Annihilationism seems compatible with some Bible verses about "destruction" or "perishing" of sinners, and it certainly fits with the statement that "the wages of sin is death" (Rom. 6:23), at least at first glance. However, other passages in the Bible refute the idea that sinners will cease to exist rather than being given eternal life. For example, Paul prophesies that "For as in Adam all die, so in Christ all will be made alive." (1 Cor. 15:22). The first "all" is the same as the second "all." *All* people die because we have the tendency of sinfulness passed on from the very first human being who walked this earth; and *all* people are going to be made alive by the renewal that comes through Christ, the redeemer of the whole world. Surely the power of sin is not greater than the power of Christ! The resurrection showed that God conquers sin and evil. Paul is saying that everyone is going to live in Christ eternally, just as everyone first has to die in Adam. That is incompatible with both eternal hell and permanent annihilation of any soul.

The Book of Revelation also contains verses that go against annihilationism. Death will be destroyed in the Lake of Fire (see Rev. 20:14). And in John's beautiful vision of eternity, he sees that "Now the dwelling of God is with men, and He will live with them. They will be His people, and God Himself will be with them and be their God.

He will wipe every tear from their eyes. There will be no more death or mourning or crying or pain, for the old order of things has passed away." (Rev. 21:3-4). God says, "I am making everything new!" (vs. 5). Sounds like both eternal hell and eternal death are ideas that John didn't believe in, so why should we?

Even the verses in the Bible that sound supportive of annihilationism actually only support the idea of temporary annihilation or a radical destruction and remaking of those who need such severe treatment, rather than a total and eternal expunging of unsaved souls from the universe. For example, Jesus talks about the wicked being burned up in Gehenna, but there is a prophecy in the Book of Jeremiah that Gehenna will someday be restored by God and will be made part of the holy city (see Jer. 31:38-40). Presumably, that would mean that everyone who was destroyed in Gehenna will someday be restored in the ultimate restoration of all things. Ezekiel prophesies that Sodom will be restored (Ezek. 16:53), even though Sodom is a symbol of God's horrible wrath and when God destroyed it with fire there was nothing said about its future restoration. Also, many verses in the Old Testament speak of God's wrath against Israel and judgments of destruction that seem final and irreversible—sometimes put in the harshest sounding terms—but the destruction of sinful Israel never proves to be complete and never-ending annihilation.

Another reason why annihilation of the wicked conflicts with the overall message of the Bible is that no soul is 100% evil. Though "all have sinned and fall short of the glory of God" (Rom. 3:23), we are nevertheless all created reflecting God's likeness, all of us being the children of Adam and Eve who were made "in the image of God" (Gen. 1:27). If something is not totally evil but contains good, then it cannot be totally destroyed. It would be God's righteous will for the good to be preserved. Therefore, no human being can be annihilated. Some parts of a personality might be destroyed in God's purging fires—maybe even a large part—but it would not be the entire essence of any person that ceases to exist.

Total and permanent annihilation would mean God giving up on the small part of an evil person that can still be saved, that God wants to save as the Father of all people. I don't believe God ever gives up on anyone. Annihilationism is no better than a halfway, feeble attempt to get out of the weighty philosophical problem of eternal hell by coming up with "hell lite"—damnation without the endless pain. God can do better than that. Let's not sell our Father short.

The Hitler Conundrum

Okay, I can accept that almost all people are saved, but what about Hitler? Ah, now we come to one of the favorite questions that just about everybody likes to raise against universalism. It is a perplexing one, and one we can all identify with. Even believers in universal salvation may be somewhat uncomfortable with the idea that people as evil as Hitler and other mass murderers could ever be saved, rather than facing eternal torment or at least annihilation.

The Hitler issue also ties in with another question: *Didn't Jesus say there is a sin that can never be forgiven?* He said, "I tell you, every sin and blasphemy will be forgiven men, but the blasphemy against the Spirit will not be forgiven. Anyone who speaks a word against the Son of Man will be forgiven, but anyone who speaks against the Holy Spirit will not be forgiven, either in this age or in the age to come." (Mat. 12:31-32). This passage actually does not describe eternal unforgiveness, nor does it refer to extremely heinous sinners such as Hitler. Jesus was warning people that if they call the work of God the work of the devil, that sin cannot be forgiven either now or in the next age. The context was that people were saying Jesus was inspired by Satan when he was doing miraculous good works, though in reality he was inspired by the Holy Spirit. If anyone should worry about committing this kind of "blasphemy against the Spirit," it is fundamentalists who have a tendency to think that any good work that is not done in Jesus' name could be secretly inspired by the devil, to deceive Christians into accepting other religions as something other than totally false and worthless. Narrow-minded religious people who see Satan lurking everywhere—who sometimes go so far as to perceive the work of God as demonic deception because it doesn't fit their preconceived notions—are the people Jesus was saying will not be forgiven of this sin for another age yet to come.

The absolute worst penalty for sin described in the Bible is for people who take the "mark of the beast." This is metaphorical imagery for following an "antichrist," an extremely evil cause involving satanic pride, a lust for power, world domination, and the persecution of righteous people. One who goes down this path "will drink of the wine of God's fury, which has been poured full strength into the cup of His wrath. He will be tormented with burning sulfur in the presence of the holy angels and of the Lamb. And the smoke of their torment rises for ever and ever [Greek: ages of ages]. There is no rest day or night for those who worship the beast and his image, or for anyone who receives the mark of his name." (Rev. 14:10-11). A lot of this language—like most of the richly symbolic and poetic Book of Revelation—is not meant to be taken literally. But the point is clear: some people are going to face an extremely long, harsh punishment for their all-consuming devotion to evil during their life on earth. People of whom it could be said that they had evil stamped upon their very being will take much longer than most for God to correct, if justice is to be served.

Does this describe a person like Hitler? Well, if it doesn't describe a man who killed millions of people in the name of pride and power-hungry madness—most of whom were the Jews, God's original "chosen people"—then who *does* it describe? It would be hard to believe that Hitler and other evil dictators are not included in the category of souls who will face "ages of ages" of suffering for their breathtaking crimes against humanity.

What will be left of Hitler after all the evil is purged out of him? After the smoke of his torment stops rising, some long ages into the future, will his soul have been almost entirely reduced to ashes? Perhaps so. But Hitler is human too, and hard though it is to believe, he was not totally devoid of goodness and redeeming qualities. God loves even the heinous criminals like Hitler, because He knows that there is still a spark of the divine within them and therefore they still have the potential to be redeemed. In fact, when Hitler one day will be saved and restored to communion with God, that will be a day of great rejoicing, because it will show God's amazing power to transform even the most evil beings into good. God will multiply the tiny spark of light in Hitler as Jesus miraculously multiplied the loaves and fishes to feed multitudes, when it didn't seem there could possibly be enough to matter.

We can speculate about how Hitler might be saved. However this process may occur, the incredible magnitude of his sins and his desperate need for atonement mean one thing for sure: He will learn to appreciate the true meaning of God's grace in a way that most people perhaps will never so intimately understand.

The Apostle Paul makes it clear that human sinfulness is all part of a larger divine purpose, which we cannot fully comprehend while we are living on earth. "For God has bound all men over to disobedience so that He may have mercy on them all. ... For from Him and through Him and to Him are all things." (Rom. 11:32,36). Paul teaches here and elsewhere in his writings that God is in control. Human beings are currently sinners because this is part of God's plan. Mysteriously, even Hitler was part of the plan; and God has plans to fix the damage he caused, including the damage to his own soul.

Yes, someday we will see people like Hitler in heaven. Thinking about that distant day, we may wish it would never come. But Jesus taught us to "Love your enemies. ... Be merciful, just as your Father is merciful. Do not judge, and you will not be judged. Do not condemn, and you will not be condemned. Forgive, and you will be forgiven." (Luke 6:35,36-37). That is the true Christian spirit. It is extremely difficult to overcome the natural human desire for vengeance, but God will help us break free from the shackles of our own pain and anger, through the power of Jesus Christ's boundless love. Vengeance is God's, and we can rest assured it will be meted out appropriately, according to the divine attributes of justice and mercy. That means no one, not even Hitler, will be forever unforgiven and remain in hell for eternity.

Don't Put Out My Fire: Christian Faith and Evangelism

By now we have answered most, if not all, of the major objections to Christian Universalism. But if universal reconciliation really is true, then do we really need Christianity? Some people might ask, *Why be a Christian if universalism is true?* A person could live life as an agnostic or a follower of another religion, because there is no awful fate in the afterlife that belief in Christ uniquely enables us to avoid. What exactly is so unique and special about the Christian faith, if it doesn't matter what religion people believe in and we're all going to the same place in the end?

I can understand why Christians might worry that their faith, or the faith of their fellow religious adherents, could be compromised or weakened by accepting universalism. But I would suggest that this problem largely originates from a lack of deeper understanding of what true Christianity is all about, and the differences between the teachings of Jesus and the teachings of other great religious founders. Jesus taught a very radical and challenging message that combines peace, love and forgiveness for all people with a strong desire for justice and the assurance that good will ultimately triumph over evil.

Some well known prophets, gurus, and religious leaders of history have also taught some of the same principles as Jesus, to be sure. Buddha's teachings about morality and the correct way of life are especially similar to what Jesus taught. But Buddha did not proclaim the existence of an all-powerful Deity who is in control of the universe and intimately, personally cares about each individual. Unlike Moses, Jesus taught freedom to act according to one's conscience rather than rigid adherence to religious laws. Unlike Muhammad, Jesus taught non-violence and the willingness to patiently endure persecution rather than the use of the sword to advance one's religious cause.

The Christian Gospel is unique among world religions, in its combination of important teachings that together can foster tremendous spiritual growth, inner peace, and the hope of peace on earth and reconciliation among enemies. Extraordinary willingness to forgive and seek brotherhood with all people, a strong conviction that our universe is ruled by a benevolent and omnipotent God who loves us with a parental love, the mystical power of the cross and the empty tomb, and a path of ever-increasing communion between ordinary people and their heavenly Father are characteristics of the faith of Christ that set it apart from all other religious faiths that have ever been created. Those are some powerful reasons to be a Christian. Eternal hell?—*who needs it!*

To conclude Part Two, let's address one final question: *Why preach the Gospel if all are saved?* Even if we are convinced that being a Christian is a good thing, better than belonging to other religions, we might lack a certain sense of urgency to "go and make disciples of all nations" (Mat. 28:19) as Jesus commanded us to do, unless we are motivated by fear for people's eternal souls.

In response, I would offer the idea that sharing the Gospel of Jesus Christ is even more wonderful and exciting when we know that what we are telling people is really Good News, not a message of fear and pessimism. Christian Universalists can go out into the world and confidently proclaim that Jesus is the savior of all people, regardless of their sins, their beliefs, or whatever other obstacles might stand in the way between them and their Creator.

On the other hand, fundamentalists who believe in eternal damnation can only tell people that God is hoping they will discover and follow the correct religious doctrines in order to escape being punished forever. That's bad news, not "good news." Before hearing this so-called gospel, most people would feel better about God, their lives and the universe than they do afterwards. The fundamentalist gospel teaches people that God is angry, vengeful, and will never forgive some people for their mistakes. Even if that were true and we go out and preach that message, most people would end up burning forever in hell anyway, so who cares if another hundredth of one percent of the world escapes such a fate? And even if a few people were to escape eternal torment by accepting the fundamentalist gospel, could we ever really be happy in heaven, knowing that the majority of the human race—probably including some of our own loved ones—are condemned to never-ending suffering?

I enjoy teaching the Gospel of universal reconciliation because I know it brings people joy, liberates them from their existential fears and insecurities, frees them from a burden of guilt in their heart, and helps them to develop a deeper relationship with God their Father in heaven. When we know that God is our Dear Father or Daddy (Aramaic: *Abba*) as Jesus taught, and we look to our Elder Brother in Christ for guidance about how to live, our spirits will grow from the size of a tiny mustard seed to a great tree where the birds will find rest, even as Jesus taught in his parable. For as Jesus said, "the Kingdom of God is within you." (Luke 17:21). The Kingdom of God is not just a place, a time, or an idea. It is a reality within us, wherever we go, whatever we do, at every moment of our lives. We only need to look within to find it, and then we are enabled to express it and manifest it.

Why preach the Gospel if all are saved? Because it is good. It is great. It is glorious. The Gospel as understood by Christian Universalists is far more wonderful than the fundamentalist bad-news gospel of eternal hell for all but a few religious believers. The Good News of universal reconciliation sets people free from a paranoid, obsessive quest to figure out exactly which doctrines they must believe and which church they must join to avoid damnation. It liberates us to focus on developing qualities that truly make us like Christ, not like the Pharisees. That's why we need to evangelize for Christ—not despite the fact that all are saved, but *because* of it! After we find the power of Christ within us, let us empower others to find it within themselves and change their life and our world for the better.

Redefining Christianity:
The Burial and Rebirth of
the True Gospel

In Part One and Two, we discussed the basic teachings of the Bible about sin, judgment and salvation, and answered the most important objections to the teaching of universal reconciliation. Now it is time for us to go deeper into the Gospel, exploring some teachings that have been hidden by the church or ignored by most Christians for centuries. The meat of the Gospel is much more amazing and revolutionary than just the promise that all people will someday be saved from their sins. When we think more deeply about the meaning of this concept, we can probably begin to imagine where it leads—but it is unlikely that most Christians ever have.

It has been so long since Christianity embraced the full implications of the Gospel, and the church has so successfully kept people distracted with side issues of religion, that some of the ideas we will be exploring may seem to be "new age" and unlike anything you ever thought could be part of the Christian faith. We will show the Biblical basis for these ideas and how they were taught by leaders of the early church before the rise of Roman Catholic hegemony and the onset of the dark ages. We will also discuss how the Catholic Church and its Protestant offshoots completely changed the substance of the Christian message and mission—mangling the faith of Christ almost beyond recognition—and how the original Gospel has gradually been revived by pioneering spiritual thinkers in more recent times.

The Nature and Essence of God

To understand the "good news" that is the Christian Gospel, we first need to understand that *God* is the beginning and end of this message. Christianity is based on belief in a benevolent Higher Being who is fully in control of what happens in the universe. Our own being and destiny is inherently tied to our relationship with God. Without God, we are nothing, and in fact nothing at all could exist.

There are certain characteristics that define the nature of the Deity and affect the laws of reality. At the core of God's essence are two important features: light and love. Light is perhaps more significant in defining who God is *in and of Himself,* without reference to other things that exist. We read in the Bible that "God is light; in Him there is no darkness at all." (1 John 1:5). Light is the most basic and essential description of God because light is energy, and energy is the very basis of existence, as modern physics attests. God is the energy source from which all creation has originated. There is no darkness in God because God is perfect and pure creative energy, and darkness (or its features, such as cold, void, and the lack of what is good) is the antithesis of God. Dark and empty space is simply the relative absence of the divine essence, the deprivation of the energy that undergirds and gives meaning and beauty to the universe. In a more metaphorical sense, darkness represents evil, so if God is light without darkness that means that God is totally good. In contrast to God, the creation contains evil intermixed with good, because created reality is a combination of both light and darkness. In creation, there really is no such thing as total darkness or total light anywhere, because all existence is sustained by the Light of God, and therefore dependent on it while being less than it.

God is light of infinite intensity and glory—not diminished in any way by darkness—and that means God is greater than everything else that exists. Although all creation is made from light energy, God's vibration, so to speak, is the highest and most powerful. No other being could ever become a greater light than God, because creation by its very definition involves separating light from darkness to create structure and diversity: greater lights, lesser lights, different patterns and colors of light, and so forth. God is "the blessed and only Ruler, the King of kings and Lord of lords, who alone is immortal and who lives in unapproachable light, whom no one has seen or can see." (1 Tim.

6:15-16). No one can see God in His/Her/Its own essence of pure and omnipotent light because comprehension of such a transcendent reality is impossible for any lesser being. Our limitations in comparison to Almighty God mean we can only see aspects of God—as much light in whatever form as we are capable of perceiving and accepting at a given time, but never the whole thing as it really is in itself. God alone is immortal in the sense that only God is self-subsisting, independent of all creation; whereas all other beings depend on God's existence, the creative and sustaining power for their own existence.

Love is the characteristic of God that is most essential in understanding God's relationship to His creation. But even if there were no creation, nothing at all outside of God, He would still be defined by love. God loves Himself. The Christian concept of the *Trinity* implies that God is capable of self-reflection and therefore self-love, because God's consciousness involves three different aspects or *personas*. Therefore God is a sentient Being, not merely an impersonal force. This is much like the way a human being has a mind, body, and spirit, giving depth and dimensionality and the capability of knowing and loving oneself. In the case of God, the triune nature is described as the Father, Son, and Holy Spirit. We have already discussed God's Fatherly nature and His incarnation as Jesus, the Son of God—and we will further explore these themes presently. But before we do, let us mention that Jesus said, "God is spirit" (John 4:24). The Spirit of God or "Holy Spirit" is the form that God takes when He interacts with people's spirits, directly influencing us through an infusion of divine light and love. The Biblical description of the Holy Spirit as "fire" alludes to God's essence of powerful light-energy that transforms creation according to the pattern God has determined.

Love is absolutely central to God's nature. "Whoever does not love does not know God, because God is love." (1 John 4:8). Even though we cannot see God in His own being as the Infinite Light, we can know Him for His love, which defines who He is. "No one has ever seen God; but if we love one another, God lives in us and His love is made complete in us." (vs. 12). By loving others, we are filled with God's Spirit, and therefore we are made holy. "And so we know and rely on the love God has for us. God is love. Whoever lives in love lives in God, and God in him. ... We love because He first loved us." (vss. 16,19). Our own capability to love derives from the fact that God is love. Because we are loved by God, we are enabled to love. In the same way that a candle cannot burn until its wick is touched by fire, we could not manifest the love of God unless God's light had first touched us. When we are infused with the power of the Holy Spirit, we gain power in our own lives to spread the light and love that is God.

The Apostle John also noted that "There is no fear in love. But perfect love drives out fear, because fear has to do with punishment. The one who fears is not made perfect in love." (vs. 18). It is not in God's nature to spread fear and terror. His creation stands in awe of His might and glory, but should not tremble in anticipation of eternal torment or rejection by God. Where there is fear, it is because of darkness—which is not of God—and it is a natural consequence of entering the darkness of sin and evil rather than abiding in the divine light and recognizing His love for all beings.

According to the Bible, "The LORD is gracious and compassionate, slow to anger and rich in love. The LORD is good to all; He has compassion on all He has made." (Ps. 145:8-9). The scriptures also tell us that "The LORD is just." (2 Chr. 12:6). Justice is actually a characteristic of love, because it serves for the ultimate benefit of all—even if it doesn't seem that way in the beginning. Contrary to the common notion that God has *competing* impulses of love and mercy, anger and justice, the truth is that justice is simply part of God's plan and the laws of His universe for bringing about the complete and perfect triumph of His love and light. If any being is in the darkness, bereft of the Spirit, God will not be satisfied until that part of creation is returned to Him. Through the exercise of the cosmic laws of justice, God reclaims that which is lost until divine love reigns in all things. Love is a pulling, drawing force whose goal is harmony and reunion—and that is *who* God is!

The Sonship of Jesus and All People

Let us now return to the theme of the Trinity. In addition to Spirit, God's nature is also described in the Bible as a Father and a Son. That's not to say that God has masculine characteristics alone. Lest we think God is *only* masculine and not also feminine, we should reflect on the fact that in the creation story in Genesis, God is said to have created human beings *both* male and female in the divine image (see Gen. 1:27).

Since women also reflect the image and likeness of God, that means that God contains characteristics associated with both genders.[7] God is sometimes portrayed as having a motherly nature (e.g. see Isa. 66:13, Mat. 23:37). However, the Bible emphasizes God's Fatherhood and the Sonship of His human incarnation, Jesus Christ.

One of the personas of God is the human form. Specifically, the Bible informs us that the historical man Jesus of Nazareth was the Christ (Hebrew: *Mashiach*, "Messiah"), who is the very embodiment of the divine essence. "For in Christ all the fullness of the Deity lives in bodily form" (Col. 2:9). That is why Christians call Jesus "Lord." Jesus Christ is described in the Gospel as the Son of God, which is a title intended to convey his special relationship and kinship with God the Father. The Son is separate from the Father in the sense that a human being is not the same thing as the Infinite Source of all being; yet in a mysterious way, it is still accurate to refer to Christ as God. Perhaps it is similar to the way a cup of water drawn from the ocean *is* the ocean, yet it is not the entire ocean. Jesus is divine, but as a human being with the limitations of a physical body, he is certainly not the whole sum of divinity. Here's another analogy: The relationship of God the Son and God the Father might be likened to the way that we can look at a painting of a man and say, "There is a man." We can even recognize who it is, if we know the subject. The painting is the image of the man, just as Paul says Christ is the "image of God" (2 Cor. 4:4).

But Jesus Christ's Sonship is more than just that. Because God is the Father, Christ as Son of God is *begotten* by God. This idea was

---

[7] Most English translations of the Bible deliberately mistranslate pronouns referring to the Holy Spirit, to conform to the traditional church doctrine of God's exclusively male gender. Proverbs chapter 8 is particularly interesting in the original Hebrew, to see the personification of the Holy Spirit as a female spirit of Wisdom that was God the Father's co-worker in creation from the beginning of the universe. The NRSV is one Bible version that preserves the feminine pronouns in this chapter. It is also worth noting that one of the Biblical Hebrew terms for God, *El Shaddai*, can be translated as "the Breasted One" or "Many Breasted God(ess)." The focus on the masculine side of God's nature in the Judeo-Christian scriptures—especially in later parts of the Bible where God is frequently envisioned as "Father"—may reflect a desire to emphasize God's role as head of household, the leader of a divine family, which was the father in patriarchal cultures.

demonstrated in a miraculous way through the virgin birth of Jesus. God brought this miracle to pass because He wanted to make the point that Jesus' Father truly was God, rather than merely an imperfect man. The point is, Jesus is perfect because his Father is perfect—and the only Father who brought Jesus into being was God Himself.

Nevertheless, we should not read too much into the title "Son of God." It was intended to set Jesus apart as especially holy, but not as totally unique. In the Old Testament, the king of Israel was also described as God's son. He even was said to have been "begotten" by God, though in a metaphorical rather than literal sense. God says, "I have set My king on Zion, My holy hill." The king of Israel responds, "I will tell of the decree of the LORD: He said to me, 'You are My son; today I have begotten you.'" (Ps. 2:6-7 NRSV). This psalm is believed to have been used on occasion of the coronation of a king. It also has significance as a prophecy of the Messiah, who will reign spiritually from Jerusalem over all the nations. It was simultaneously a statement about God's special relationship with the Hebrew king of the day, and with the spiritual King who was yet to come, who came as Jesus and manifested the fullest reality of the concept of a begotten Son of God.

God as Father does not only apply to God's relationship with Jesus. Far from it! God says, "I have found David My servant; with My sacred oil I have anointed him. … He will call out to Me, 'You are my Father, my God, the Rock my Savior.' I will also appoint him My firstborn, the most exalted of the kings of the earth." (Ps. 89:20,26-27). But not only King David was regarded as God's firstborn son. Long before he ever received this title, Adam was the son of God—and as the first man on earth, he was the archetype of all men. Unlike other men but like Jesus, Adam had no earthly father. The difference is that Adam fell into sin whereas Jesus overcame it. But that doesn't change the fact that Adam is also regarded as God's offspring. In the New Testament, this archetypal ancestor of the entire human race is referred to as "the son of God" (Luke 3:38). The implication is that since we are all descended from Adam, we all are in some way the children of God.

"Have we not all one Father? Did not one God create us?…" asks the prophet Malachi (Mal. 2:10). The Apostle Paul answers the question: There is "one God and Father of all, who is over all and through all and in all." (Eph. 4:6). Paul preached in a sermon to the Athenians that God "is not far from each one of us. 'For in Him we live and move and have our being.' As some of your own poets have said, 'We are His offspring.'" (Acts 17:27-28).

The word used in Greek for "offspring" in this verse is *genos*, which implies the relationship of a father begetting a child. Paul could have chosen a Greek word indicating only physical creation such as one might make an object, but instead he specifically decided to use a word conveying the idea of generation, kinship, same-species birth. By affirming the belief of the Athenian poets and philosophers that humans are intimately related and connected to God—not mere creatures like the animals but in fact the very kin of God, sons and daughters of the Spirit—Paul is stating a truth that may strike many Christians today as radical and revolutionary. But this was clearly taught as an important theme of the Gospel in the early church. This idea fits naturally with the teaching in Genesis that Adam and Eve, the first parents of the human race, were made in the image of God and therefore all human beings are God's descendents bearing His divine resemblance. Somehow, this essential Biblical concept has largely escaped the notice of most Christians for hundreds of years.

If sonship is not only for Jesus but for all people, then that means we are all to be like Jesus, manifesting the light and love of our heavenly Father God who is "the Father of our spirits" (Heb. 12:9). Jesus teaches us to "love your enemies, do good to them, and lend to them without expecting to get anything back. Then your reward will be great, and you will be sons of the Most High, because He is kind to the ungrateful and wicked." (Luke 6:35). Jesus said to crowds of people in his famous Sermon on the Mount, "You are the light of the world." (Mat. 5:14). *Imagine that!* How often do we hear traditional Christian ministers preaching that the divine light is not only limited to Jesus but also resides in *us*? Jesus continues: "A city on a hill cannot be hidden. Neither do people light a lamp and put it under a bowl. Instead they put it on its stand, and it gives light to everyone in the house. In the same way, let your light shine before men, that they may see your good deeds and praise your Father in heaven." (vss. 14-16). We are called to openly manifest our sonship even as Jesus did, not hiding it for fear that people may think us arrogant to believe we are the offspring of God. Jesus makes it clear that when we do what is right and good, we are showing our true nature and living up to our station as children of the Divine Light.

Jesus also said, "I am the light of the world. Whoever follows me will never walk in darkness, but will have the light of life." (John 8:12). He said, "When a man believes in me, he does not believe in me only, but in the One who sent me. When he looks at me, he sees the One who sent me. I have come into the world as a light, so that no one who believes in me should stay in darkness." (John 12:44-46). When we call Jesus the Light, we are recognizing that the light of God within him is stronger than our own—even though Jesus said we can also be the light of the world. Knowing Jesus as the perfect Light who came into this world that is filled with darkness means that we understand our need to follow one who has more light than we do, so that we, too, can learn how to be filled with light and spread it to others until the whole world may be filled with God's Spirit of light and love.

Jesus warned that he was going to die and ascend to his Father, and that after that it would be more difficult for people to follow his path because they would not be able to see his living example. He instructed people to follow him earnestly while he was alive on earth, so that they could learn how to become like him to manifest the divine light as children of God: "The light [Jesus] is with you for a little longer. Walk while you have the light, so that the darkness may not overtake you. If you walk in the darkness, you do not know where you are going. While you have the light, believe in the light, so that you may become children of light." (John 12:35-36 NRSV). Being a disciple of Jesus Christ means coming into the knowledge of our own sonship, and developing and practicing our capability of living according to the way of light that Jesus showed during his earthly incarnation.

Indeed, discipleship means both recognition of our station as well as action to live accordingly, which is often difficult. Because we are the children of Adam in addition to the children of God, we also have the fallen Adamic nature within us, not only the divine nature. We must struggle to overcome these sinful tendencies and learn to live according to the spirit (Christ) rather than the flesh (Adam). This means rejecting the temptations of darkness and evil we are prone to fall into, and embracing the spiritual path of Christ. "For you were once darkness, but now you are light in the Lord. Live as children of light (for the fruit of the light consists in all goodness, righteousness and truth) and find out what pleases the Lord." (Eph. 5:8-10). Our transformation from darkness to light, from our fallen inheritance of corruption and death in Adam to our glorious station of sonship and eternal life in Christ, is a process of awakening to our true potential for which we were originally created. When the morning of spiritual rebirth arrives—at a time and in a way that is different for each person—God says, "Wake up, O sleeper, rise from the dead, and Christ will shine on you." (vs. 14).

The Fall and Resurrection of Human Nature

If we are all the children of God, why does acting in a godly way not come naturally to us? Why are we living in darkness and need to be restored to our true selves? Why did the first man, Adam, rebel against the way of God and become the father of a fallen race of men? Couldn't God have prevented this, and ensured that Adam and his descendants would only be inclined toward good and never evil?

These are profound philosophical questions that go to the root of the nature of God's plan and the very purpose of existence. In the Biblical accounts of creation, we read the story of the forbidden fruit— the fruit of the tree of knowledge of good and evil—which Adam and Eve ate in defiance of God. They were tempted by the promise of immortality and godhood which is the fruit of divine knowledge. But in receiving this knowledge of good and evil, light and darkness, they took something that they were not yet ready for and could not handle. It was like a young child seeking to learn about things suitable only for an adult to know. This resulted not in instant maturity, but loss of innocence and a time of suffering. These natural consequences are represented in the story by Adam and Eve's expulsion from the simple and serene Garden of Eden, the nursery of mankind, and into the larger world with all its excitement and trouble. Man got what he asked for! He wanted knowledge, and he got it along with all its implications, both positive and negative.

God wasn't going to keep us in the Garden of Eden forever. One day, Adam and his descendants would have been let out of the metaphorical playpen. But perhaps the development of humanity would have happened in a more gradual, less turbulent way, without all the bitter fruits of premature knowledge. As soon as man rebelled against God and could no longer stay in a state of blissful ignorance and ease, evil began to rear its ugly head. We read in Genesis that immediately following the sudden departure from Eden, man began to descend into wickedness: jealousy and hatred, brother killing brother, tribal divisions, and all other manner of corruption. Things got so bad that "The LORD was grieved that He had made man on the earth, and His heart was filled with pain." (Gen. 6:6).

So man was fallen into darkness. Though we were created in light, we rebelled because we *wanted* knowledge of dark things. The craving for such knowledge and experience of things *other* than God and His light was what set humanity on the path of sin and destruction. We would have to experience judgment in order to be restored.

It is inevitable that any child will rebel against his parents, whether it happens sooner or later. To some degree, this is a necessary learning process. Children cannot grow into mature adults unless they experience what it is like to make mistakes and learn from the consequences. That is the reason why God did not stop man from rejecting His authority and following the path of sin. By respecting human free will and allowing us to do wrong and face the resulting judgments, God was actually showing His desire for people to be more than mere automatons. The plan is not for robotic obedience, but for the development of a true desire and appreciation for the ways of our Father, which can only come about by discovering the misery and shame of the alternative.

Human nature is resurrected after the fall into sin through the process of judgment and salvation. The Bible tells this story throughout its pages. "My son, do not despise the LORD's discipline and do not resent His rebuke, because the LORD disciplines those He loves, as a father the son he delights in." (Prov. 3:11-12). Punishment is not for vengeance, but for purging of evil and ultimate healing and reconciliation: "Blessed is the man whom God corrects; so do not despise the discipline of the Almighty. For He wounds, but He also binds up; He injures, but His hands also heal." (Job 5:17-18). And as Job so beautifully put it, "when He has tested me, I will come forth as gold." (Job 23:10).

Even though the fall of man was the result of free will, it was also part of a greater plan not of our own choosing and understanding.

God explains that He is the master of all creation: "I form the light and create darkness, I bring prosperity and create disaster; I, the Lord, do all these things." (Isa. 45:7). God said He would allow the people of Israel to fail to perceive and heed His warnings for a period of time, so that they could experience harsh judgments and punishments for their sins (see Isa. 6:9-12). This was part of God's plan for their full redemption and restoration, and indeed their transformation to a higher degree of glory.

The same sort of plan is in effect for all people, with the goal of all God's children rising through adversity and tests into the foreordained destiny of mature sonship. "The creation waits in eager expectation for the sons of God to be revealed. For the creation was subjected to frustration, not by its own choice, but by the will of the One who subjected it, in hope that the creation itself will be liberated from its bondage to decay and brought into the glorious freedom of the children of God." (Rom. 8:19-20).

Christ is the key to God's plan for humanity. Jesus' resurrection from the grave is a powerful sign of the potential for liberation and glorious divine immortality latent within all of us. We only have to learn how to tap into this potential and make it a visible reality. All of us as the descendents of Adam are imperfect, but our destiny is to be made new in the image of Christ—not only some of us, but *all* of us, as the scriptures declare. This destiny was anticipated from the very beginning of the divine plan, and the fall of man could not stop it—because even despite our fall into sin, God has the remedy in Christ. Since we are created in God's image, our sins cannot forever define who we are. Since we are all to be resurrected with Christ, the mistakes of the race of Adam shall one day pass away, replaced by Christlike perfection.

But before we can experience this resurrection, first we must go through a crucifixion. As Paul said, "I have been crucified with Christ and I no longer live, but Christ lives in me. The life I live in the body, I live by faith in the Son of God, who loved me and gave himself for me." (Gal. 2:20). To become sons of God like Jesus Christ, we must embrace the purifying judgments of God and die to this world. We must do as Jesus said: "If anyone would come after me, he must deny himself and take up his cross daily and follow me." (Luke 9:23). "And anyone who does not carry his cross and follow me cannot be my disciple." (14:27).

If we strive for discipleship and live in the self-sacrificial spirit as Jesus lived, "we know that our old self was crucified with him so that the body of sin might be done away with, that we should no longer be slaves to sin… [C]ount yourselves dead to sin but alive to God in Christ Jesus." (Rom 6:6,11). Christians are taught to "put off your old self" and "put on the new self, created to be like God in true righteousness and holiness." (Eph. 4:22,24). "Be imitators of God, therefore, as dearly loved children and live a life of love, just as Christ loved us and gave himself up for us as a fragrant offering and sacrifice to God." (5:1-2).

Suffering is part of the purgatorial process that leads to maturity and glorification. Paul says that "The Spirit Himself testifies with our spirit that we are God's children. Now if we are children, then we are heirs—heirs of God and co-heirs with Christ, if indeed we share in his sufferings in order that we may also share in his glory. I consider that our present sufferings are not worth comparing with the glory that will be revealed in us." (Rom. 8:16-18). Our spiritual inheritance is truly great. But to receive it, we must become like Jesus Christ, who like us was a descendant of Adam but resisted temptation, accepted divine judgment that he didn't even deserve, and conquered the Adamic nature of sin and replaced it with the divine nature of righteousness. He has inherited all things as God's firstborn Son, and we will inherit with him as soon as we are ready.

God thought we were ready 2,000 years ago! Humanity had come through phases of development under the law, like a child who must obey rigid rules set by parents. But that time was coming to an end and man was growing up. Paul described the unfolding of God's plan for His human offspring, saying "as long as the heir is a child, he is no different from a slave, although he owns the whole estate. He is subject to guardians and trustees until the time set by his father. So also, when we were children, we were in slavery under the basic principles of the world. But when the time had fully come, God sent His Son, born of a woman, born under law, to redeem those under law, that we might receive the full rights of sons." (Gal. 4:1-5). We are called to move beyond the immature, childish stage of bowing down to a Lord and receiving punishments for our sins, and rise into the inheritance of spiritual adulthood.

Paul says that "all of us" are supposed to come "to maturity, to the measure of the full stature of Christ. … [W]e must grow up in every way into him who is the head, into Christ" (Eph. 4:13,15 NRSV). He says that "the word of God in its fullness—the mystery that has been kept hidden for ages and generations, but is now disclosed to the saints… is Christ in you, the hope of glory. We proclaim him, admonishing and teaching everyone with all wisdom, so that we may present everyone perfect in Christ." (Col. 1:25-28).

Greek Orthodox Christians call this concept *theosis*, which means "becoming divine" or divinization. The idea is that Christians are to become perfected like Christ as the mature sons of God, so that he will be more like an elder brother to us than a Lord. Accepting Jesus as Lord is only the first step of salvation, not the last as many Christians erroneously believe. If we continue to grow in the salvation process, we will mature past the need to bow down to Jesus as a Lord, in the same way that an apprentice outgrows the initially exaggerated reverence for his master. Eventually, a more collegial and less authoritarian relationship can develop. As Jesus said, "A student is not above his teacher, but everyone who is fully trained will be like his teacher." (Luke 6:40).

If we have Christ as our teacher, then someday we will be just like Christ. That's not some new age heresy; it's what the Gospel promises. We are not to remain in spiritual kindergarten forever, but as students of Christ we are to learn from him until we attain a similar station, graduating from the elementary levels of life to a higher divine calling. As children of God the Father, we are not to stay childish, but to grow up into a Christlike maturity even as Christ perfectly embodied the essence of divinity as the Son of God.

Divine Potential of Man Revealed through Christ and the Saints

Some people have been specially called by God to be co-workers with Christ in this age of creation, before all will be reconciled and restored to glory. As Christ was chosen by God to show others the way of salvation, so too are Christians given this calling as brothers of Christ, manifesting his image. That's why even though God is the "Savior of all men," this is true "*especially* of those who believe." (1 Tim. 4:10). God already knows who is going to believe and walk in the path of Christ before they are even born in this world. "For those God foreknew He also predestined to be conformed to the likeness of His Son, that he might be the firstborn among many brothers." (Rom. 8:29).

Saints—those people who follow the path of Christ as his true disciples—are set apart for a glorious purpose in which not all souls will yet participate. They are called to intercede on behalf of sinners and help show them the way out of hell, as Jesus did and surely still does. Paul describes the life and mission of the saints: "[I]f anyone is in Christ, he is a new creation; the old has gone, the new has come! All this is from God, who reconciled us to Himself through Christ and gave us the ministry of reconciliation: that God was reconciling the world to Himself in Christ, not counting men's sins against them. And He has committed to us the message of reconciliation. We are therefore Christ's ambassadors, as though God were making His appeal through us." (2 Cor. 5:17-20). Paul is explaining that true Christians, who have received salvation already and are remade in the image of Christ, are specially chosen by God to share the Good News of universal reconciliation with everyone else and lead people back to God so that they, too, can become like Christ.

The gates of hell are locked from the inside, and the Gospel is all about encouraging people to open the door of their hearts to their heavenly Father and let Him in. Christianity is supposed to be a "message of reconciliation," and adherents to the faith of Christ are supposed to minister to people by focusing not on their sins but on their divine potential. As John says, "How great is the love the Father has lavished on us, that we should be called children of God! And that is what we are!… and what we will be has not yet been made known. But we know that when [Christ] appears, we shall be like him, for we shall see him as he is. Everyone who has this hope in him purifies himself, just as he is pure." (1 John 3:1-3).

In the age to come, the saints "will be priests of God and of Christ and will reign with him for a thousand years." (Rev. 20:6). This special group of people are those who became disciples of Christ during their life on earth. They are called "the first resurrection," because they have been raised up from the life of corruption to a higher level of being before everyone else. Their goal is to work with Christ to accomplish God's larger purpose of restoring all people and all things to a blessed state.

"You have made them to be a kingdom and priests to serve our God, and they will reign on the earth," prophesies John (Rev. 5:10). These saintly souls leave heaven and return to earth not for the aionian chastisement, but for the aionian life of glory and power. Through their presence here, they will transform this world into the paradise of justice, righteousness, and universal love and brotherhood that numerous prophets have dreamed of and written about in the scriptures. The Kingdom of God will finally be visibly established on earth, after centuries of waiting and longing for it while we have lived in a corrupt and wicked world. Some of the saints will "take charge of ten cities" and others of fewer (Luke 19:17-19), according to how worthy their service to God has been during ordinary life. "Do you not know that the saints will judge the world?... Do you not know that we will judge angels?" says Paul (1 Cor. 6:2-3). Yes, the people who have proven themselves fit for this station will be given authority formerly reserved only for God Himself.

These glorious prophecies about the future role of saints may be understood either literally or in a more poetic and mystical sense. My own opinion is that the details do not really matter; what is clear is that human beings are called to participate intimately in the process of the reconciliation of all things, both now and in ages to come. People who demonstrate in their lives that they are effective servants in God's cause will ascend into a station of great spiritual power, and will continue to assist—in ever more meaningful and responsible ways as part of the Heavenly Father's household—to accomplish the goals of the divine plan.

Very few people have even begun to comprehend what we will become when we are in Christ. John hinted at it, and so did Paul. God says bluntly, "You are gods, children of the Most High, all of you; nevertheless, you shall die like mortals…" (Ps. 82:6-7 NRSV). Jesus confirms that this statement is in reference to human beings, not to mythological pagan gods as many interpreters of the Bible choose to believe. He says to the Jews who were accusing him of blasphemy for calling himself the Son of God, "Is it not written in your Law, 'I have said you are gods'? If He called them 'gods,' to whom the word of God came—and the Scripture cannot be broken—what about the one whom the Father set apart as His very own and sent into the world? Why then do you accuse me of blasphemy because I said, 'I am God's Son'?" (John 10:34-36). Jesus goes on to say that "the Father is in me, and I in the Father." (vs. 38).

Jesus prays to God for his followers, "that all of them may be one, Father, just as You are in me and I am in You. May they also be in Us…

I have given them the glory that You gave me, that they may be one as We are one: I in them and You in me. ..." (John 17:21-23). Jesus is saying that those who follow him will also attain a state of glorification and oneness with God, by being filled with the Spirit of Christ and living in harmony with the divine. Jesus continues his prayer, saying, "Righteous Father, though the world does not know You, I know You, and they know that You have sent me. I have made You known to them, and will continue to make You known in order that the love You have for me may be in them and that I myself may be in them." (vs. 25-26). Jesus is emphasizing his station as the manifestation of God in this world, and our potential to become one with Christ by manifesting the love of God ourselves.

There is no limit to our potential to manifest divine qualities. Jesus makes this remarkable statement: "Very truly, I tell you, the one who believes in me will also do the works that I do and, in fact, will do greater works than these..." (John 14:12 NRSV). *We* could someday do *greater* works than Jesus?—unthinkable! But it's not heresy if Jesus said it, and he did say it, right there in the Bible. Obviously, no human being can even do works as great as Jesus did, currently. A few people on this planet might perhaps be able to miraculously heal the sick, but we are unable to give sight to the blind, walk on water, feed multitudes with one loaf of bread, literally raise the dead and rise from the dead ourselves in bodily form. But someday that will change, if Jesus' words are to be believed. Jesus promises that by following him, we will be able to ascend to a spiritual level where we will have powers we could only dream of during ordinary life today. "I tell you the truth," he says, "if you have faith as small as a mustard seed, you can say to this mountain, 'Move from here to there' and it will move. Nothing will be impossible for you." (Mat. 17:20). It may take long ages of growth and development, but before the end of time we can truly become like Jesus and attain powers worthy of gods, as Jesus called us all. The saints, practicing discipleship, will reach this point sooner and will show the way for others, as Christ did first.

Christians should not be shy about openly affirming such ideas. We may be reticent and hold back our proclamation of these amazing truths of the Gospel for fear of being labeled heretics, new age kooks, dreamers, or some other term of derision. But we are called to share the light, not conceal it. Paul alluded to the way Moses covered his face which was shining with the divine light when he returned to the people of Israel after communing with God. He criticized the Jews for following in this spirit of concealment, saying that "their minds were made dull" and "a veil covers their hearts" (2 Cor. 3:14,15). Christians, Paul says, should be "very bold" (vs. 12), not veiling their glory or the glorious message of the Gospel but letting the divine light shine. It is God's will for people to manifest the image and likeness of God. "And we, who with unveiled faces all reflect the Lord's glory, are being transformed into His likeness with ever-increasing glory, which comes from the Lord, who is the Spirit." (vs. 18).

Restoration and Reunion of All Beings—Life on Earth

At some point in the vast eternity before the present time, every one of us came out from God's inapproachable, incomprehensible Light as tiny flaming sparks of spirit and descended into the universe, which undoubtedly contains many different realms and dimensions of existence. Now we have incarnated into a physical body on the planet we call "earth," which we often erroneously believe to be our home— but if we understood our true spiritual origin and divine nature as the offspring of God, we would realize we are "aliens and strangers in the world" (1 Pet. 2:11) and would seek to return home to the Light from which we originated.[8]

Nevertheless, all of this is a necessary process of separation, experience and learning, and the development of an individual perspective on reality. If we had never left the innermost court of the Divine Presence, we could never have become unique individuals contributing ever-increasing richness to the canvas of creation. Our lives in the universe, separated to some degree from God, weave diverse and colorful threads in the tapestry of existence, expanding and infilling it with the realization of specific aspects of infinite potential. When we someday return to oneness with God, it will not be the extinction of individuality, an empty *nirvana* that swallows up souls in a uniform and meaningless bliss; it will be something far more wonderful, a veri-

---

[8] There are verses in the Bible which indicate that human spirits preexist incarnation into a physical body. For example, God says to Jeremiah, "Before I formed you in the womb I knew you" (Jer. 1:5).

table unity in diversity in which we become like the cells of one body, the Body of Christ, united while remaining individuals. Nothing valuable that we have experienced in our journey of separation from God shall be lost!

We are all like the Prodigal Son—both as individual spirits and the human race collectively—because we have *all* fallen and left the Father's house. No human being alive on earth is yet perfect. That will come later as the destiny of all people to grow up into Christ and attain reconciliation with the Father, returning to our true home in God's Kingdom. "[W]hen perfection comes, the imperfect disappears. When I was a child, I talked like a child, I thought like a child, I reasoned like a child. When I became a man, I put childish ways behind me. Now we see but a poor reflection as in a mirror; then we shall see face to face. Now I know in part; then I shall know fully, even as I am fully known." (1 Cor. 13:10-12).

We find ourselves on earth because God saw fit to put our spirits in this realm. Right now, we are not fit for heaven. It may be that this planet is like a school for the developing human soul, and when we learn our lessons and pass, we go on to a higher level of existence in a heavenly plane, closer to God. When we fail, we find ourselves in the temporary punishment of a hellish state. Perhaps then we may be required to "repeat a grade."

One question that many people ask about universalism is how the souls of the wicked are reformed. How does this process actually work? Early Christians held a great diversity of views about the nature of the afterlife, so this was a subject of much debate. Among universalists in the early church, many believed that earth itself is an upper level of hell through which fallen souls must pass on the way back to heaven. Some discussed the possibility that a spirit could live more than one human life on earth as a way to become perfected and return ever closer to God. They found support for this concept in the Bible: James, the brother of Jesus and leader of the Church in Jerusalem, penned a classic description of how sin, such as wrongful speech leading to evil actions, is the driving force for the "cycle of nature" or "wheel of birth" (Jas. 3:6 NRSV). The Greek term he used in the original text was a common term describing reincarnation in Greek philosophy. At the time, both Jews and Greeks were open to the idea that coming to earth for multiple lives could be part of the divine plan for human existence. The apostles said that people who heard of Jesus were speculating that he might be the return of the prophet Elijah or another prophet such as Jeremiah (see Mat. 16:13-14). Some also interpreted Jesus' controversial teaching that John the Baptist was Elijah as a reference to reincarnation (see Mat. 11:13-15, 17:12-13).

These ideas have been blotted out of the Christian religion over the centuries, and today, most Bible versions try to obscure the presence of reincarnation in the early Christian tradition through deliberately faulty translations. It is important to note, however, that Biblical evidence on the subject is mixed, and not all early Christians agreed with this idea. Even those who did always limited its scope specifically to multiple *human* lives—not the Hindu concept in which a person might come back as a lower species of animal.

Regardless of one's beliefs about how the afterlife works, what really matters is that God knows what's best for each and every soul He has created. I believe that God will put us wherever we need to be at any particular time—whether on earth or in hell or somewhere else unknown—until we have reached the full stature of divinity that we were created to reflect and manifest in our lives. When we finally do reach that point, perhaps that is the meaning of the resurrection, the state of being in which sin and death can no longer have any power and one's soul-identity shall remain eternally preserved.

No one wants to be here in this earthly place of imperfection and struggle instead of the peace of heaven. But despite its problems, the realm of earth is meant to exist for a purpose, and God says its creation is "very good." (Gen. 1:31). There is much beauty in the earthly realm alongside the suffering and sorrows, and it seems as though throughout the history of human existence on this planet after the Fall, the higher powers have always maintained a delicate balance between good and evil on earth. This gives humans the ability to choose various directions while we are living here. This cannot be just a coincidence, but seems to have great significance as a program for the winnowing and refinement of character. Earth may be a very unique and special place for the growth of souls.

As the souls of human beings grow closer to divine perfection, earth should come to resemble heaven more than hell. Jesus Christ instructs us to pray to our heavenly Father, "Your kingdom come, Your will be done on earth as it is in heaven." (Mat. 6:10). Christ is the cornerstone of the divine plan. Jesus speaks of "the renewal of all things, when the Son of Man [Christ] sits on his glorious throne…" (Mat. 19:28). He says that at that time, "many who are first will be last, and many who are last will be first" (vs. 30), but he does not mention anyone being left out completely. The renewal and regeneration will extend to all beings, until all are eventually made one in Christ.

Peter also speaks of this renewal of all creation in one of his sermons, calling it "the time of universal restoration that God announced long ago through His holy prophets." (Acts 3:21 NRSV). Let's look at some of those Old Testament prophecies. In the Psalms, it says that "All the ends of the earth shall remember and turn to the LORD; and all the families of the nations shall worship before Him. … [B]efore Him shall bow all who go down to the dust… Posterity will serve Him; future generations will be told about the LORD, and proclaim His deliverance to a people yet unborn, saying that He has done it." (Ps. 22:27,29-31 NRSV). "O You who hear prayer, to You all men will come. When we were overwhelmed by sins, You forgave our transgressions." (Ps. 65:2-3).

The prophet Isaiah envisioned a time when "the LORD Almighty will prepare a feast of rich food for all peoples, a banquet of aged wine… He will destroy the shroud that enfolds all peoples, the sheet that covers all nations; He will swallow up death forever. The Sovereign LORD will wipe away the tears from all faces; He will remove the disgrace of His people from all the earth. The LORD has spoken. In that day they will say, 'Surely this is our God; we trusted in Him, and He saved us. This is the LORD, we trusted in Him; let us rejoice and be glad in His salvation.'" (Isa. 25:6-9). Isaiah also wrote these moving words that have inspired countless souls to look forward to a day of peace on earth and brotherhood of all people: "In the last days the mountain of the LORD's temple will be established as chief among the mountains; it will be raised above the hills, and all nations will stream to it. … He will teach us His ways, so that we may walk in His paths. … He will judge between the nations and will settle disputes for many peoples. They will beat their swords into plowshares and their spears into pruning hooks. Nation will not take up sword against nation, nor will they train for war anymore." (2:2-4). Micah echoes this same prophecy in his own book (see Mic. 4:1-3).

There are even visions of miraculous changes in the natural world, made possible by the abundant presence of the Holy Spirit: "The wolf will live with the lamb, the leopard will lie down with the goat, the calf and the lion and the yearling together... The infant will play near the hole of the cobra, and the young child put his hand into the viper's nest. They will neither harm nor destroy... for the earth will be full of the knowledge of the LORD as the waters cover the sea." (Isa. 11:6,8-9). This is not all necessarily literal, but the prophecy speaks to the idea of a restored and improved natural order. People, too, will be different. God promises, "I will pour out My Spirit on all people." (Joel 2:28). Human civilization will be regenerated to a state of perfect justice and righteousness, under the leadership of Christ. The Messiah will have "authority, glory and sovereign power; all peoples, nations and men of every language worshiped him. His dominion is an everlasting dominion that will not pass away, and his kingdom is one that will never be destroyed." (Dan. 7:14).

The Bible also teaches that before the visible establishment of God's Kingdom on earth, first there will be an apocalyptic time of trouble, during which evil will rear its ugly head for one last triumph before finally being defeated. This difficult transition will be like the "birth pangs" of a new era (Mat. 24:8 NRSV). However, we are cautioned not to try to predict when these things will happen, because even Jesus himself says that *he* doesn't know! "No one knows about that day or hour, not even the angels in heaven, nor the Son, but only the Father." (Mat. 24:36). Only God knows the timetable and details of the divine plan for the transformation of our world.

Restoration and Reunion of All Beings—No One Excluded

One of the most important prophecies in the Old Testament concerns the covenant God made with Abraham. God said to the great patriarch Abraham, "in you all the families of the earth shall be blessed." (Gen. 12:3 NRSV). This was an unconditional promise that God made, and we know that God is true to His word. Therefore, we can be confident that in the ultimate restoration of the world that is coming, all people will enter into a state of blessing rather than condemnation. The vast majority of families of human beings who have ever lived never had a single member who was a Christian. Yet they will be blessed anyway, because the power of Christ to save souls does not depend on our religious beliefs. God says, "Turn to Me and be saved, all you ends of the earth; for I am God, and there is no other. By Myself I have sworn, My mouth has uttered in all integrity a word that will not be revoked: Before Me every knee will bow; by Me every tongue will swear." (Isa. 45:22-23).

We need to understand the monumental import of this statement in scripture. *Every* knee will bend before the Lord and *every* tongue confess His divine authority—not only humans, but all beings "in heaven and on earth and under the earth" (Phil. 2:10)—in other words, the entire creation. This will be "to the glory of God the Father" (vs. 11), rather than the forced submission of still-rebellious souls tormented in hell. The clear implication is that even demons and evil spirits—and yes, even the devil himself—can eventually be saved. At the end of the ages, the Spirit of Christ will "fill the whole universe" (Eph. 4:10).

Paul says, "For as in Adam all die, so in Christ all will be made alive. But each in his own turn. ... For he must reign until he has put all his enemies under his feet. ... When he has done this, then the Son himself will be made subject to Him who put everything under him, so that God may be all in all." (1 Cor. 15:22-23,25,28). "As in Adam all die" refers to spiritual death, the fall of man which also brought death of the body, mind, and soul. "In Christ all will be made alive" refers to a total spiritual rebirth, the resurrection of the whole person without exceptions. "Each in his own turn" means that some people will be reborn before others: first the true Christians who pattern their life after Christ, and then other people later. Some people will be saved during their earthly life, while others will not be saved until after physical death. Eventually Christ will conquer *all* of God's enemies in the entire universe, both human and non-human, and transform them from a life of sin and rebellion to the new life in Christ. The ultimate goal is for God to be "all in all," meaning that the Holy Spirit of God will abide and abound in all beings. Paul states this as a prophecy, not a mere possibility.

Christians are privileged to know this amazing and wonderful outcome of God's plan while it is still a long time in coming. "He made known to us the mystery of His will according to His good pleasure, which He purposed in Christ, to be put into effect when the times will have reached their fulfillment—to bring all things in heaven and on earth together under one head, even Christ. In him we were also chosen, having been predestined according to the plan of Him who works out everything in conformity with the purpose of His will, in order that we, who were the first to hope in Christ, might be for the praise of his glory." (Eph. 1:9-12). This passage describes the way God has saved true followers of Jesus through predestination and grace, for salvation in this life according to God's will. Furthermore, it states that God's will always becomes a reality in due time, and that His will and "good pleasure" is for all people to be brought together under the leadership of Christ. Paul emphasizes over and over again that this *will* be accomplished, in the same way God predestined the Christians to be the first people to believe in Jesus. Saying that the Christians are the "first" to praise God's glory also implies that there will be others who have not yet experienced salvation, but will become part of the body of Christ at a later time.

Becoming one with Christ means a total transformation of one's being, liberation from the separation and division that is the chief characteristic of the fallen state. Paul says to the followers of Christ, "you have taken off your old self with its practices and have put on the new self, which is being renewed in knowledge in the image of its Creator. Here there is no Greek or Jew, circumcised or uncircumcised, barbarian, Scythian, slave or free, but Christ is all, and is in all." (Col. 3:9-11). If he were writing today, he could have also said there is no black or white, male or female, "Christian" or "heathen," even human or extraterrestrial. All are one in Christ. Returning to God, all distinctions that have separated and divided us melt away in the fire of God's universal light and love. We will remain unique individuals, while becoming one in the greater whole of the Divine Being. This ultimate goal of mystical reunion of all beings with God through Christ—no matter how far we may have fallen and how separated we have become from the Light in which we were created—is what it means for God to become "all in all."

We dream of the day when, after long ages in darker realms—often not even able to perceive the Light of the Spirit in our lives—we will finally be reunited with the Source of our being, letting our light shine in perfect harmony with the great Lamp of creation. In the meantime, we look forward to a coming age in which our world will be restored, becoming more like the kingdom of heaven and less like the hell on earth that generations of humans sadly have known. With an unfailing hope, we pray that these things are coming soon, knowing that the dreams of great prophets and saints shall indeed become a reality in the fullness of time. This knowledge and the joy it brings is the Good News, the true Gospel, that believers in Christ are commissioned to share with an aching world.

Church Fathers Who Taught the True Gospel

Now that we have seen what the Biblical Gospel teaches, it is important that we understand how Christianity came to be such a very different religion—so different, in fact, that much of the Gospel as we have presented it would be unrecognizable to the majority of Christians and regarded by many as a deliberate misinterpretation of the Bible and a new age heresy. The next few sections will provide a broad outline of the development of Christian thought and the institution of the church, beginning with the time immediately after the Apostles and the authors of the New Testament and proceeding through medieval times and up to the present day. We will discover that far from being a new invention, the Gospel we have shared is the original Gospel taught by the greatest early church theologians. It was only later, after the church became worldly, corrupt, and filled with pagan and imperial traditions, that Christianity became something we are more familiar with, which is less consistent with the message of the Bible.

The first point worth noting is that universalism was the prevailing view of salvation in the early church. In Greek, it was called *apokatastasis*, the restitution of all things; and this was a mainstream teaching of Christianity. The concept of eternal damnation to a tormenting hell was largely unheard of among Christians in the first century—especially those of a Jewish background, who knew this was not taught in the Hebrew scriptures—and it only gradually came to be believed by some Christians in the second and third centuries as more Gentiles from a Greco-Roman background converted to the faith of Christ, bringing some of their pagan ideas along with them. The most influential competitor to universalism in the early church was actually annihilationism, the view that eternal life is conditional and the wicked will simply die as mortals, never to live again. Annihilationism and eternal conscious torment both gradually gained ground, though Christians who held to these exclusive views of salvation were in the minority through the third century.

We know this to be the case because of textual evidence from early Christian sources, such as the Church Fathers who wrote about and taught the faith as the most important leaders of Christian thought in their time. Many of these influential men discussed the divine plan for the ultimate restoration of all things. For example, Saint Irenaeus the Bishop of Lyons (130-202 C.E.) and Saint Theophilus the Bishop of Antioch (died circa 185) both left behind significant statements in their writings that attest to their belief that all will eventually be saved through God's redemptive judgment. It is particularly noteworthy that St. Irenaeus wrote a lengthy book called *Against Heresies*, but never once mentioned universalism as a heretical belief.[9]

The greatest exponents of universalism in the early church were based in the Egyptian city of Alexandria, the center of learning and intellectual culture for the entire ancient world. This cosmopolitan metropolis was the meeting place of philosophers, theologians, writers, teachers and students of various belief systems, and during the first three centuries of Christian history it became the most important city in the Christian world. Saint Clement of Alexandria (150-220) was the first great father of the church to arise from this climate of higher education and scholarly discourse. Nevertheless, he also had a direct connection to the Apostles of Jesus Christ, having studied Christianity with one of their disciples. The mixture of unadulterated oral tradition he received from the earliest Christians and his Greek philosophical foundation and intellectual ability made St. Clement of Alexandria a uniquely significant figure. On the issue of salvation, St. Clement wrote:

> "For all things are ordered both universally and in particular by the Lord of the universe, with a view to the salvation of the universe. But needful corrections, by the goodness of the great, overseeing judge, through

---

[9] Hanson, J. W. *Universalism: The Prevailing Doctrine Of the Christian Church During Its First Five-Hundred Years*. Chapter 6. Boston: Universalist Publishing House, 1899. Republished online at http://hellbusters.8m.com/updcontents.html and http://www.tentmaker.org/books/Prevailing.html

the attendant angels, through various prior judgments, through the final judgment, compel even those who have become more callous to repent. ... So He saves all; but some He converts by penalties, others who follow Him of their own will, and in accordance with the worthiness of His honor, that every knee may be bent to Him of celestial, terrestrial and infernal things (Phil. 2:10), that is angels, men, and souls who before his [Christ's] advent migrated from this mortal life. ... For there are partial corrections (*paideiai*) which are called chastisements (*kolasis*), which many of us who have been in transgression incur by falling away from the Lord's people. But as children are chastised by their teacher, or their father, so are we by Providence. But God does not punish (*timoria*) for punishment (*timoria*) is retaliation for evil. He chastises, however, for good to those who are chastised collectively and individually."[10]

St. Clement's student and successor was Origen (185-254), the greatest early Christian theologian and church father. Origen began his work in Alexandria, was ordained as a priest in Greece, and later founded a school at Caesarea, the provincial capital of Palestine. He wrote the first systematic commentary and exegesis of the entire Bible, including concordance, and he produced a Bible in six columns, showing parallel versions of the Greek and Hebrew text. His greatest contribution was to develop a comprehensive understanding of the Biblical Gospel that was based on belief in God's plan for the ultimate redemption and restoration of all as the foundation of the Christian message. Origen died as a martyr, enduring torture at the hands of the Roman government for his faith in Christ, during a time of great persecution of the Christian community.

Most of Origen's copious writings have been lost or destroyed, but what remains shows a picture of a spiritual thinker almost unparalleled in the depth of understanding he demonstrated concerning the Bible, the nature of God and humanity, and the divine plan of ascent

---

[10] *Stromata*, VII, ii; *Pedagogue*, I, 8; on I John ii, 2. Quoted in Hanson. Ibid. Chapter 9.

and reunion of all beings with their Creator through successive ages and trials. Origen wrote concerning the way God will restore all beings to Himself:

> "God's consuming fire works with the good as with the evil, annihilating that which harms His children. This fire is one that each one kindles; the fuel and food is each one's sins. ... When the soul has gathered together a multitude of evil works, and an abundance of sins against itself, at a suitable time all that assembly of evils boils up to punishment, and is set on fire to chastisement... [I]t is to be understood that God our Physician, desiring to remove the defects of our souls, should apply the punishment of fire. ... Our God is a 'consuming fire' in the sense in which we have taken the word; and thus He enters in as a 'refiner's fire' to refine the rational nature, which has been filled with the lead of wickedness, and to free it from the other impure materials which adulterate the natural gold or silver, so to speak, of the soul. [O]ur belief is that the Word [Christ] shall prevail over the entire rational creation, and change every soul into his own perfection. ... For stronger than all the evils in the soul is the Word, and the healing power that dwells in him; and this healing he applies, according to the will of God, to every man."[11]

After Origen, two other significant Christians of the ancient world who believed in universalism were Saint Gregory of Nyssa and Saint Macrina the Younger, who were brother and sister. St. Gregory of Nyssa (335-394) was a bishop and theologian. He was much influenced by Origen's religious views, but made notable contributions of his own to the development of Christian theology. Gregory's main issues of interest were the Trinity, the nature of God, and God's plan for humanity. One of his most significant teachings is the idea that God is infinite and beyond any limited human understanding. Another is his teaching of *epektasis*,

---

[11] *De Principiis*, II, x: 3, 4. I, i. *Against Celsus*, iv, 13; VIII. lxxii. Quoted in Hanson. Ibid. Chapter 10.

the constant progress of human beings toward greater and greater levels of divine perfection. The combination of this idea with the infinite transcendence of God was an important development in the Christian belief in *theosis* (divinization of man through spiritual growth).

St. Macrina the Younger (324-380) was a nun who founded a sisterhood of several hundred women, and is honored as one of the most prominent nuns of the Eastern Church. Her grandmother was St. Macrina the Elder, also a universalist. Macrina the Younger was well educated and well versed in scripture, and was a supporter of Origen's teachings. She was an avowed believer in the salvation of all, and believed that the resurrection is the restoration of human nature to its pristine condition of harmony with the divine. Macrina was known for her skill as a manager of her family and religious community, her life of piety and force of character.

Other prominent Christian Universalists of the ancient world include Saint Pantaenus (d. ca. 216), who founded the theological school in Alexandria where St. Clement and Origen later taught; Saint Didymus the Blind (313-398), who headed this school for half a century and invented a system of reading for the blind based on letters carved into wood (a precursor to Braille), which enabled blind students to study the scriptures; and Bishop Theodore of Mopsuestia (350-428), one of the founders of the Nestorian Church which still exists today as the Assyrian Church of the East.

Most people do not realize that Christian Universalism has a solid history in the early church, and was in fact the predominant view of the Gospel for the first few centuries of the history of Christianity. The controversial ideas we have discussed, as well as the basic belief in universal reconciliation, date back to the time of the Apostles and Church Fathers of ancient Christian faith. Origen, for example, was a believer in all major aspects of the interpretation of Christianity presented in this book, and he was regarded as the greatest Christian thinker of his era and a serious Bible scholar. Today, we are only rediscovering the original message of the Gospel as expounded by its earliest believers, not creating a brand new theological system. These are timeless truths that seem new to us today, not because they are recently invented, but simply because they have been suppressed by institutional religion for so long—to the point that people have forgotten what Biblical Christianity is really supposed to be.

A Different Gospel: The Rise of Roman Church Tradition

Perhaps the most important event in Christian history after the crucifixion and resurrection of Jesus Christ was the conversion of the Roman Emperor Constantine (272-337), who legalized Christianity in the Roman Empire in the year 313 and became a patron of the Christian clergy. Christianity quickly went from a persecuted minority group to the dominant and semi-official religion of Rome because of Constantine's support. But along with this dramatic improvement in status came increased infighting among Christians who believed in different versions of the faith. Constantine sought to resolve these conflicts by calling an ecumenical council of bishops to decide Christian orthodoxy. Religious freedom of conscience for Christians would be a thing of the past.

The result of these changes was that Christianity came to have a much more Roman orientation, because Rome was involving itself in Christian affairs through government power. Knowing that the Roman Empire—formerly the arch-enemy of the Christian faith—would play a role in determining what type of Christian beliefs and practices would be considered normative or heretical, Christian leaders increasingly sought to please the state and ensure their position rather than seek truth. A politicization of Christianity thus took place over the coming centuries, with the end result that church and state became closely united with the development of the papacy as a powerful governing institution. The bishop of Rome assumed the title *Pontifex Maximus*, which was originally a title used by the Roman emperor, and is still used today to refer to the Roman Catholic pope who presides over the church from Rome. Christianity and Roman imperial traditions became thoroughly merged.

One of the side effects of the shifting center of gravity of Christianity from Alexandria and Palestine to Rome was that the Bible increasingly came to be read in Latin translation, rather than the original Greek and Hebrew. This allowed for distortions of the scriptures to be seen as part of the Judeo-Christian message. Tragically, the most important church theologian after Origen was a man who converted to Christianity from a pagan background after the development of the post-Constantine Christian empire, who *could not even read Greek* and thus had no command of the language in which the New Testament was written and in which the early Christians had read the Bible. This theologian was Augustine (354-430), considered the father of all Western theology. He was responsible for a wholesale change in Christian thinking, replacing the belief system of the Apostles and most of the early Church Fathers with a completely different version of the gospel that has been handed down to us as the fundamental basis of Catholic and Protestant Christianity. Only the Eastern Orthodox churches reject Augustine and have preserved the use of the Greek Bible and at least some of the Hellenistic interpretation of the Christian message rather than the later Latin ideas that usurped the Gospel.

Augustine was the turning point in the development of Western church-approved theology because he enunciated the central concepts of the religious paradigm that took hold in the middle ages and persisted in large part to the present day. His most important ideas which are contrary to the Biblical Gospel include, first and foremost, the belief that the very essence of our being is evil, because humans are defined in God's eyes by our "original sin" that is passed on as a sexually transmitted disease at birth, and therefore damnation is the default destiny of all people—even unbaptized babies who die in infancy—because of God's furious anger. Secondly, he taught that hell is eternal and anyone who is not saved from divine condemnation during life on earth will experience eternal conscious torment. Along with this idea is the teaching of predestination by God of some people to heaven and all others to hell, not because of their works either in this life or any past existence, but because of arbitrary favoritism. The cornerstone of Augustine's religious system was the belief in the necessity and unique power of ritualistic church sacraments and priests for people to attain salvation from hell, based on the concept of "created grace" that can be dispensed only by the Roman Catholic Church. Cementing the whole system together was a strong support for the authority of the church hierarchy and organization as the "visible kingdom of God on earth," and its role in law, politics, war, and government—including the punishment of heretics.

The development and spread of this perverse, unbiblical Augustinian theological system was bad enough, but it was reinforced in future centuries by further key events, which combined to force Christianity as a whole to repudiate many of its original teachings and serve a completely different function from what it was originally intended to be. One of these was the official declaration that hell is eternal by the Roman Emperor Justinian in the year 544. Another important event was when Origen was officially declared a heretic in 553. The legacy of the greatest early church theologian and his illuminating writings were thus cast out of the church, and with this travesty the destruction of original Christian theology and its replacement by Roman Church tradition was virtually complete.

The only major piece of the puzzle that remained to be put in place was the assertion of the papacy as supreme and unchallengeable in all matters—an idea that had gradually been developing in the West but was resisted by the East, leading to the Great Schism in which the Eastern churches broke away from Roman authority in 1054. Thomas Aquinas (1224-1323), one of the most significant Western church theologians, emphasized and further developed the concept of papal supremacy and absolute authority of the centralized church, strengthening the iron grip of the religious hierarchy on people's souls throughout Catholic Europe. Nowhere in the Bible is such a rigid system of church power prescribed. In fact, evidence from the New Testament reveals that several apostolic leaders (Peter, Paul, James, and John) shared influence in a collegial arrangement. But a dictatorial church, based upon Roman imperial ideals that were foreign—even hated—by the early Christians, would triumph as the culmination of the creation of a new, pseudo-Christian religion that hijacked the name of Jesus Christ.

Some other important ideas developed by the Roman Catholic Church during these centuries of the decline of the original Christian Gospel include the notion that God and man are totally separate and different in nature; we are only creatures, not children of God. A corollary of this unbiblical teaching is that Jesus as the "only Son" will forever be Lord, to whom we must grovel and plead for mercy from his Father's unquenchable wrath, and humans can never become like Christ and rise into the station of divine sonship. These ideas are the rejection and antithesis of the Eastern Orthodox concept of *theosis*, which is absolutely central to the Biblical Gospel as taught by the Apostle Paul and expounded by the greatest early church theologian, Origen, and which remains an important concept in Eastern Orthodoxy today (though in a weakened and diluted form). In the middle ages, the Western church truly developed a different gospel, focused on appeasing God's hatred of the lowly human race by performing sacramental rituals—a stream of religious thought and practice that bears little resemblance to the early church and was Christian in name only.

Catholicism, Protestantism, and the Crimes of Pseudo-Christianity

Jesus warned about false prophets, who claim to speak for God and represent the truth but who are really spreading evil. "They come to you in sheep's clothing, but inwardly they are ferocious wolves. By their fruit you will recognize them. … [E]very good tree bears good fruit, but a bad tree bears bad fruit." (Mat. 7:15-17).

Much of the fruit of the tree of Christianity has been foul. Aggressive wars, brutal tortures and murder of numerous people with different beliefs, and other heinous crimes were committed in Jesus' name, by an institution calling itself the Church and by those who most ardently supported it. And it was not just the Catholics! After the Reformation, Protestants and their churches also participated in unholy acts that defiled the name and obscured the message of Christ.

The "Dark Ages" of medieval times were dark because the light of the Gospel went out, replaced by false gospels that held people in bondage to fear of the devil and demons who seemed to have more power over our salvation than God, and the threat of eternal hell for anyone who dared question the beliefs or transgress the laws of the church. Even in the somewhat more enlightened East, Christianity was corrupt enough that it could not compete with the spread of a mighty and ascendant Islam on the only terrain where the Christian faith has a clear advantage—the inner battlefield of the heart. Thus, Muslim armies conquered much of the formerly Christian world with the power of the sword, backed by a new religious text, Muhammad's Quran, that spoke more convincingly than a decadent church that had distorted the hopeful and glorious message of its own Bible. Meanwhile, in the West, the masses were plunged into the darkness of superstition and blind obedience to a clerical hierarchy that denied their inner light and freedom of conscience.

The Crusades are a salient example of the distortion of Christian teaching. The non-violence of Jesus and the Apostles was replaced by an Islamic-style reliance on military might as the way to spread and establish religion. Jesus' command to "Put your sword away!" rather than fight for religious reasons (John 18:11) was ignored as Roman popes called upon Christian men across Europe to march to the Holy Land with swords in hand to fight the Muslim infidels. After a short-lived victory for the church, the Muslims won the war mainly because their own religious tradition was not conflicted on this matter; it fully embraced the sword as legitimate and God's way of holiness[12]—whereas Christianity was going against much of its own scripture and tradition on this issue, and therefore was destined to lack confidence and sufficient will-power to sustain the cause once it became impractical. In the process of fighting the Crusades, which ultimately accomplished nothing, Christians slaughtered many innocent people, raped women, burned cities, and sowed indiscriminate destruction—all in the name of the Lord Jesus Christ, who had explicitly prohibited the use of violence to promote his religion.

Back home in Europe, torture and execution for heresy were becoming an integral part of Christianity, imposed by the "Holy Office" commonly known as the Inquisition. The main reason for these practices was to prevent the spread of ideas—theological, scientific, philosophical or political—that could undermine the absolute authority of the church and cause people to lose their salvation and be condemned to eternal hell because of wrong belief. Also, it was hoped that those being tortured or burned at the stake might recant their heretical beliefs and profess renewed allegiance to the church before death, saving their souls from hell. Ironically, the main purpose these practices *really* served was to enable thousands and thousands of "heretics" to die

---

[12] Many verses in the Quran (also spelled Koran) proclaim the glory of *jihad* (holy war), and the religious duty of all able-bodied Muslim men to take part in it. For example: "Fighting is prescribed for you…" (Quran 2:216). "Fight those who believe not in God nor the Last Day, nor hold that forbidden which hath been forbidden by God and His Apostle [Muhammad], nor acknowledge the religion of Truth [Islam], even if they are of the People of the Book [Jews and Christians], until they pay the Jizya [tribute] with willing submission, and feel themselves subdued." (9:29). "God hath purchased of the believers their persons and their goods; for theirs in return is the garden of Paradise: they fight in His cause, and slay and are slain… then rejoice in the bargain which ye have concluded: that is the achievement supreme." (9:111).

as martyrs for Christ, much as Jesus was unjustly executed on a Roman cross. The Roman Catholic stake became the symbol of a church that had completely and utterly divorced itself from anything that was truly of the Holy Spirit—having become, like the authoritarian and expansionist Roman Empire of New Testament times, an infernal engine of evil and corruption in this world.

With Martin Luther (1483-1546) and the coming of the Protestant Reformation in the sixteenth century, there was hope that Christianity might rediscover its roots and abandon many of the unbiblical beliefs and practices it had developed. Luther and other reformers did succeed in establishing new churches free from papal authority and some of the most notorious examples of corruption, such as the sale of "indulgences" that exploited people's fear of hell to fatten the coffers of the clergy. However, the theological underpinning of Luther's theology was flawed, because he overemphasized the importance of doctrinal belief as a substitute for the works-oriented sacramental religiosity of the Catholic Church that he rightly rejected. Luther taught that salvation comes from divine grace *by faith alone*, meaning that it became even more important for people to decide exactly what was the correct way to believe. The predictable result was a rapid multiplication of Protestant sects based on competing formulas of the "one and only true faith" and therefore which Christians are saved and which are damned.

Protestants fought among themselves for converts, and they also fought with the Catholics who sought to retain exclusive control over the Western Christian world. In the Thirty Years War, from 1618 to 1648, more than 20% of the population of Germany is estimated to have perished as a result of the fighting and its effects—a war that started because Catholics and Protestants could not live with each other in peace. Such were the bitter fruits of a religion that had developed increasingly narrow ideas about salvation and taught that most people were going to a hell of eternal torment simply because they might not have all the right theological beliefs. They had no tolerance to allow people to believe and worship God in their own way, even if they all agreed that Christ is Lord.

We become like the God we worship. If we worship a cruel God, we will be cruel. If we worship a vengeful God, we will take revenge on those we see as His enemies. If we worship a sadistic God, we will delight in tormenting those who do not worship Him or who disagree with our religious views. It's only natural for people to emulate the characteristics of their God, whether they do so deliberately or sub-consciously. The Catholic queen of England, "Bloody" Mary (reigned from 1553-1558), burned nearly 300 Protestants to death at the stake. She said, "As the souls of heretics are hereafter to be eternally burning in hell, there can be nothing more proper than for me to imitate the divine vengeance by burning them on earth."[13]

In the more recent age of colonialism by Christian nations, vast numbers of people in the Americas, Africa, and other remote regions of the world were persecuted or slaughtered in the name of Christ, all because they refused to convert or bow down to their Christian masters. As in the Crusades, these things were done despite the fact that Jesus himself opposed the efforts of Jewish zealots who sought to establish God's kingdom on earth through the power of the sword. Aggressive colonialism was inspired in large part by the desire to save all the peoples of the world from eternal hell by converting them to Christianity—by force if necessary—and to purge the world of people that God supposedly hates and condemns because of their pagan be-liefs. If God was going to give them hell and torture them forever any-way for refusing to profess allegiance to the "true religion," why not get the process started a little bit earlier?

Christians have historically been encouraged to do almost anything necessary to save souls from damnation and bring them into the ex-clusive fold of the church, including mistreatment of non-Christians, military conquest of territories, even torture and bloodshed. The un-derlying reason for these abuses was a warped view of who God is and who we are. The Gospel had been crucified on the cross of Roman Catholic tradition and buried in the tomb of darkness and forgotten. Instead of the Good News of God's loving Fatherhood and the destiny of all people to be saved and patterned after His firstborn Son, Jesus Christ, people who called themselves Christians only knew a gospel of terror and hatred. They had been taught by the churches to believe in

---

[13] Thayer, Thomas B. *The Origin and History of the Doctrine of Endless Punishment*. Chapter 7. Boston: Universalist Publishing House, 1855. Republished online at http://hellbusters.8m.com/origincontents.html and http://www.tentmaker.org/books/OriginandHistory.html

a God who, as Calvinist preacher Jonathan Edwards thundered in an infamous eighteenth century sermon, "holds you over the pit of hell, much as one holds a spider, or some loathsome insect over the fire, abhors you, and is dreadfully provoked: his wrath towards you burns like fire; he looks upon you as worthy of nothing else, but to be cast into the fire; he is of purer eyes than to bear to have you in his sight; you are ten thousand times more abominable in his eyes, than the most hateful venomous serpent is in ours."[14]

Catholic priest J. Furniss wrote about hell in a religious book for children: "The little child is in this red hot oven. Hear how it screams to come out. See how it turns and twists itself about in the fire. … You can see on the face of this little child what you see on the faces of all in Hell—despair, desperate and horrible! … God was very good to this child. Very likely God saw that this child would get worse and worse, and would never repent, and so it would have to be punished much more in Hell. So God, in His mercy, called it out of the world in its early childhood."[15] This child, however, would never be released from God's torture chamber according to church doctrine; it was only mercifully blessed with a fire somewhat less hot than more seasoned sinners. With ideas as sick as these, no wonder the world itself was a hellish place!

Revival of Universalism in Modern Times

The Roman Catholic Church still has not yet apologized for most of the barbaric atrocities and crimes against humanity it committed in Jesus' name. However, God is ready to forgive, and one of the signs of God's willingness and plan to restore all things is that the Catholic Church has made great progress in the modern era toward a less harsh, more loving spirituality. Even the church that did the most to destroy Biblical Christianity can still be restored and reconciled with its millions of victims, by changing its ways and coming to God's truth. Much credit

---

[14] Edwards, Jonathan. "Sinners in the Hands of an Angry God" (1741). Available online at http://en.wikisource.org/wiki/Sinners_in_the_Hands_of_an_Angry_God

[15] Furniss, Reverend J. *The Sight of Hell: A Catholic Book for Children* (1870). Quotations republished online at http://www.mrdankelly.com/hell.html

must be given to pioneering popes such as John XXIII and John Paul II who did much to refocus the Catholic mission and message and make it more universalist in spirit and practice, if not fully in doctrine.

Many Protestant churches have also moved away from the focus on hell and an exclusive view of salvation in recent decades. There has been a growing trend of ecumenical dialogue and the hope of eventual reconciliation of the many denominations of Christianity. Both Catholics and Protestants have also made strides toward overcoming anti-Semitism, which was formerly a potent force in Christian theology, as well as some genuine attempts to understand various non-Christian religions and appreciate their value and the dignity of their adherents as God's children.

But long before these things began to happen in the latter half of the twentieth century, there was already a burgeoning movement toward full-blown Christian Universalism, the belief in God's redemptive judgments and the ultimate salvation of all people. In the middle ages, only a few scattered mystics and visionaries had dared to profess belief in universalism—brave, freethinking, and saintly souls such as Johannes Scotus Erigena (815-877), Johannes Tauler (1300-1361), Blessed John of Ruysbroek (1293-1381), and Blessed Julian of Norwich (1342-1416). As the Reformation came into full flower and the institutional church was put on the defensive by an outpouring of spiritual radicalism, three new denominations emerged which taught universalism: the Anabaptists, the Moravians, and the Quakers. Hans Denck (1495-1527) was a German theologian and Anabaptist leader who advocated universalist ideas. Bishop Peter Boehler (1712-1775) spread the Moravian teaching of universalism from central Europe to England and the American colonies; and his influence helped John Wesley (1703-1791), the founder of Methodism, to become sympathetic toward the idea of universal reconciliation in his later years. William Penn (1644-1718) founded the state of Pennsylvania as a haven for persecuted Quakers, bringing universalist beliefs and a spirit of open-mindedness into the heady brew of religious debate in early America.

Revolutionary Christian thinkers in the eighteenth and nineteenth centuries continued the process of questioning church tradition about salvation and damnation, seeking a better, more Biblically accurate and philosophically reasonable way of understanding God's plan for dealing with the problem of sin than the typical Catholic or Reformed theology. Many ministers, writers, and theologians from diverse denominational and geographical backgrounds advocated various types of Biblical Universalism instead of the traditional belief in eternal conscious torment. Some of the most important and recognizable names of the early modern era include William Law (1686-1761), James Relly (1722-1778), George de Benneville (1703-1793), Elhanan Winchester (1751-1797), John Murray (1741-1815), Hosea Ballou (1771-1852), Friedrich Schleiermacher (1768-1834), J. W. Hanson (1823-1901), George MacDonald (1824-1905), Hannah Whitall Smith (1832-1911), and Karl Barth (1886-1968).

Others too numerous to mention contributed greatly to the advance of Christian Universalist belief, writing books and preaching sermons to spread the idea of a God too good to condemn anyone forever, our heavenly Father who sent Jesus Christ to be the savior of *all* the world. Famous people who believed in or sympathized with Christian Universalism include U.S. President Abraham Lincoln; Clara Barton, founder of the American Red Cross; Florence Nightingale, pioneer of modern nursing; and Benjamin Rush, a signer of the Declaration of Independence.

The Universalist Church of America was created in 1793, and for nearly a century it was a large and influential denomination with many congregations, ministers, authors, and prominent members. However, this church failed to adapt to changing times and lost its evangelical spirit. In 1961, it merged with the American Unitarian Association to form the Unitarian Universalist Association (UUA). With this merger, the only Christian Universalist organization of churches died an ignoble death and was largely forgotten. The UUA does not affirm basic Christian teachings, and Christians have been leaving this organization over the past few decades as it has drifted into secular humanism.

Many Christians today are unaware of the rich ecclesiastical history of universalism as a Christian movement and do not realize that it's possible to be a Christian and a universalist at the same time—even though universalism was the original Christian teaching about salvation, and it was revived into public consciousness within the past couple centuries. Though the betrayal of Biblical Christian principles by both Catholic and Protestant churches was dramatic and overwhelming, Christianity can still be resurrected to glory from the tomb of false tradition. It need not merely become a watered down version of the traditional church system, refusing to talk about hell while refusing to eliminate this stain upon its creed.

In fact, some denominations today are beginning to go beyond the middle ground of avoidance of the topic of hell, taking the first tentative steps into the realm of open profession of Christian Universalism. For example, in 1995 the Church of England Doctrine Commission wrote in an official report, *The Mystery of Salvation,* that it is "incompatible with the essential Christian affirmation that God is love to say that God brings millions into the world to damn them." The same report encouragingly states that "Over the last two centuries the decline in the churches of the western world of a belief in everlasting punishment has been one of the most notable transformations of Christian belief."[16]

Another major denomination, The Evangelical Lutheran Church In America, has an article posted on its official website which quotes modern Lutheran theologian Carl Braaten in support of universal reconciliation: "ELCA Lutherans will say with Braaten… 'Salvation is what God has in store for you and me and the whole world in spite of death, solely on account of the living risen Christ. … The universal scope of salvation in Christ includes the destiny of our bodies together with the whole earth and the whole of creation. … This hope for the final salvation of humanity and the eternal universal restitution of all things in heaven and on earth … is drawn from the unlimited promise of the Gospel and the magnitude of God's grace made known to the world through Christ.'"[17]

The Liberal Catholic Church goes even further in affirming a belief in the salvation of all. This group arose in the early 1900's as a mixture of ideas from the Theosophy movement and the Old Catholic Church, a German and Dutch sect of Catholics that broke away from Rome because they did not believe in the newly announced Roman Catholic

---

[16] "The Mystery of Salvation, The Story of God's Gift: A Report by the Doctrine Commission of the General Synod of the Church of England." London: Church House Publishing, 1995. p. 180; p. 199.

[17] "Telling the Lutheran Story, FAQs: Salvation." http://www.elca.org/questions/Results.asp?recid=21. Quoted text from Braaten, Carl, "The Universal Meaning of Jesus Christ," *LCA Partners Magazine*, December 1980 and June 1981.

doctrine of papal infallibility. The statement of faith of the LCC Province of the USA (one of the two most significant organizations or sects of the Liberal Catholic movement) expresses some key universalist beliefs: "We believe that God is Love, and Power, and Truth, and Light; that perfect justice rules the world; that all His sons shall one day reach His feet, however far they stray. We hold the Fatherhood of God, the Brotherhood of man..."[18]

These progressive Christian denominations, and others such as the United Church of Christ and the Disciples of Christ (Christian Church) which lean increasingly in a universalist direction, have however been shy about openly and strongly teaching the salvation of all people as a central focus of the Gospel. But a surprising and exciting development during the 1990's and early 2000's is the emergence of a rapidly growing belief in universal reconciliation among more conservative Christians, especially independent Pentecostals as well as some Evangelicals. This activity has been prolific on the internet, and in the context of informal conferences and meetings of like-minded ministers and believers.

Future developments may or may not include one or more new denominations. It is likely that the existing denominations with universalist leanings will become more open about this and will emphasize it more in their teaching. If they don't, then that would increase the likelihood that new denominations could form with an explicitly universalist focus, because progressive Christians who take their spirituality seriously are not interested in a wishy-washy church with the trappings of traditional religion but no overarching theological message. My hope is that denominationalism and a hierarchical, creedal view of Christianity will diminish—as will the "empty shell" churches coasting on established name recognition that no longer have any serious spiritual message to proclaim—and a new spirit of unity in diversity and open-minded fellowship will flourish, based on the Christian Universalist spirit of all-inclusive love grounded in basic Biblical principles. I believe the emerging house church movement will play a major role in the development of such an authentic, deeply principled yet broad-based Christianity for the twenty-first century.

_____

[18] "Basic Tenets of the Liberal Catholic Church." http://members.tripod.com/~LiberalCatholic/tenets.htm

The Christian Universalist Association was founded in 2007 by myself along with several other ministers, evangelists, professors and writers who believe in Christian Universalism. We hope to lead an ecumenical movement to bring together churches and individuals around the world from a variety of backgrounds and traditions, to make the universalist understanding of the Gospel once again a mainstream view of the Christian faith, and a major spiritual option available to all people.

Conclusion

Effects of Our Beliefs about Salvation

Imagine if you really, *really* believed that most people are headed for hell, never to be released from an everlasting torment, because they have the wrong religious beliefs to obtain God's forgiveness for their sins. What would you do about it? How would you live your life? Would you go about your ordinary business, working eight hours a day in a regular job and enjoying the recreational pleasures of a middle-class existence? Would you talk about sports and lawn care with your atheist or Buddhist neighbor, instead of the terrifying message of your religion? If so, you would be an uncaring hypocrite. Yes, that may sound harsh, but think about it.

If the Ruler of the universe really is so merciless and unforgiving that he demands us to find the one and only true religion to escape a fiery doom, then it is everyone's responsibility as a compassionate human being to spend *every waking hour* warning people about the threat of eternal hell. Moreover, any act that will spare a person from this horrific destiny in the afterlife would be a righteous action—even if it is profoundly unjust, even evil, by human standards. Getting in people's faces, disturbing the peace and shouting over and over again that "Jesus is the only way to be saved!" is tame in comparison to the actions that would be expected of us according to basic principles of morality, if eternal hell is true. Saving even one individual from this fate would trump all other considerations, because according to the fundamentalist creed, hell is an *infinite* and *unbearable* punishment. No amount of earthly suffering, madness and mayhem would be enough to relieve us of our moral duty to *live a hell-centered life*, focused entirely on saving souls from hell by any means necessary.

Frankly, if eternal hell is the destiny of most people—or even a *possible* destiny for anyone—then it would be criminal to bring new children into this world. Who would be so callous as to risk creating a being that could someday end up being tortured for endless ages? Mere reproduction, a basic human instinct, becomes a heartless and fearsome act in the context of belief in the traditional Christian doctrine of damnation. The birth of every new baby, instead of a cause of celebration, would be an event of sorrow and horror, for we would hear in the precious infant's cries the echo of future shrieks of agony that would go on for billions and trillions and infinite numbers of years in hell.

Andrea Yates, the criminally insane mother who drowned her five young children in a bathtub, committed this absurd and heinous act because she was afraid if they grew up beyond the "age of accountability" they might become possessed by demons and go to eternal hell. According to the logic of fundamentalism, she should be celebrated as a hero. After all, she may well have prevented souls from entering the agonizing, perpetual flames of God's wrath, and ensured their place in heaven.

Jesus defined the purpose of his mission without any reference to saving people from eternal hell: "The Spirit of the Lord is on me, because He has anointed me to preach good news to the poor. He has sent me to proclaim freedom for the prisoners and recovery of sight for the blind, to release the oppressed, to proclaim the year of the Lord's favor." (Luke 4:18-19). Why can't Christians take their Lord at his word? As Paul said, "For the grace of God has appeared, bringing salvation to all" (Tit. 2:11 NRSV).

Now imagine that *this* is what you believed. Imagine yourself with a deep and abiding faith in God's plan of salvation for all people, believing that everyone in the world is your brother or sister in God's family and that He loves each and every one of us with a parental love—a love that can never fail. Imagine that you could see the face of Christ reflected in the face of every person you meet, and that someday that person will be with you in heaven, worthy of great honor and praise, cleansed of all sin and patterned after Christ, your Lord.

If you *really* believed this, just imagine how happy you would feel, and what a blessing you could be to others. Every mistake or problem in life could be seen as an opportunity for growth, not a chance to put someone down or count someone out—or to give up and count yourself out. God is a God of second chances, as many chances as we need to get it right. He is a God who never gives up on anyone—and that includes you. It also includes the homeless man on the street, the woman in the mental ward, the kid born in the ghetto who sought to escape through drugs and petty crime, and even the hardened criminal in maximum-security prison. It includes the ones who, burdened by injustice and anguish and the harshness they have known, have denied God, denied any real meaning in life, denied human dignity, and denied their own divine nature within because they were never told it was there. It includes the billions of people who have lived and died without knowing God and repenting of their sins. They, too, shall someday walk beside us in the Kingdom. No power in the universe, neither sin nor death, can prevent God from saving our souls, according to His magnificent and triumphant plan. We may struggle to remain in the hell of disbelief and rebellion, but eventually God will win us over and we will become who we were meant to be: mature children and heirs of our heavenly Father.

What a wonderful hope! Imagine the positive difference such high expectations—of our God and ourselves—can make in our lives, in our world. With a powerful faith in the Good News of Christ and the inner peace it brings, you *can* make a difference. It's time to stop imagining, and start working to make God's plan of universal redemption and reconciliation a reality. Our beliefs do matter. They make us who we are.

A Hell-Shaped Hole in Our Heart

Because of centuries of pseudo-Christian church tradition ingrained in the collective consciousness of our society, many Christians live with a repressed fear of God. Only the true fundamentalists actually talk about hellfire and damnation anymore. Most are unwilling to confront the issue so directly. And for good reason. It is a terrible thing to think about, and it causes many people to question their faith. So in most churches, people ignore the unpleasant, unspeakable doctrine of eternal hell. It hangs over the congregation like a thin but ever-present cloud of fear, floating around, potentially striking anyone at any time. For most Christians, most of the time, its only effect is to dull the joy of their faith, subtly undermining the spiritual growth they seek by polluting their soul with a lingering doubt that never quite gets resolved.

Sometimes, however, the fear of a condemning God breaks through and envelops a soul, choking it half to death. This usually happens during times of crisis and uncertainty in life, when everything seems to be going wrong, our prayers don't seem to be getting answered, and we wonder if God really cares about us—or if He's up there at all. At such times, we may find ourselves questioning our salvation. We may become angry at God, and we ask Him why He lets bad things happen to good people. And then we find ourselves face to face with the ogre that has been staring at us all along from the shadows: the grim idea of damnation. If God can let bad things happen to good Christians, just imagine how much worse He must be to the sinners and unbelievers! Maybe the fire-and-brimstone fundamentalists really are right! Filled with sadness and anger at the misery God allows in His universe—both on earth and beyond the grave—we tremble in fear of an angry God, cowering before our master like a kicked dog and begging his forgiveness for real and imagined sins. The good news of Christianity has become something else, and it begins to burn a hell-shaped hole in our heart.

For some people, this hole was already burned long ago, perhaps in their childhood. They were raised in a church that emphasized the curse of sin and its terrible consequences: eternal rejection by God and permanent imprisonment in a place of pain without hope of forgiveness. Or they converted to such a belief out of fear of what could happen otherwise. *"Abandon all hope, ye who enter here!"* shout the tracts and the slogans. *"Thousands of degrees hot, and not a drop of water!"* Isn't that, after all, what the Bible teaches? There's no escape from the gospel truth, just like there's no escape from hell. Or so they say. Countless little children grow up scared of a ferocious judge on a throne in the sky who is counting all their sins against them, rather than trusting in our Father who is in heaven. Jesus called God our *Abba*—literally "Daddy" in the Aramaic language he spoke. But what kind of a daddy locks some of his children in a closet for the rest of their life? And what kind of a God maintains an eternal hell? Certainly not a God we can call "Daddy." Oh, the confusion!

No wonder so many people who grow up in fundamentalist churches end up as atheists, or as spiritually confused and miserable Christians. No wonder there is so much depression, anxiety, and stress-related illness today. We live in a fast-paced time of great change and uncertainty with problems like nuclear weapons and terrorism; and as if that weren't enough, we cannot even trust in the unfailing love and benevolence of our own God. Is God a terrorist? Does He really say, "Convert or be tortured in My cosmic dungeon for eternity"? Is God a child abuser? Does He really say, "Obey or your heavenly Father will beat you bloody until you cry for mercy—and then some more"? I sure hope not. Praising the Lord just wouldn't be the same.

God Drew Me Out of Darkness: A Testimony

I was fortunate enough not to have been taught to fear the sadistic God of fundamentalism when I was a child. So the damage to my heart was not done at an early age, when it can be seared into a person in a way that is much harder to heal. For me, the hell-shaped hole was burned in later, after I converted to Christianity. It came when unfortunate events in my life caused me to begin losing faith in God and Christ, and I started meditating on who the God of Christianity really is, and how He works in this world and the worlds of the afterlife. As a compulsive seeker of truth, I could not help but try to find a resolution to my religious doubts and fears.

I was brought up without religion and spent much of my youth searching for something to believe in beyond the ordinary things of this world. After experimenting with different religions and philosophies, I finally accepted Jesus Christ as my Lord at the age of 23. I accepted him because I knew I needed forgiveness for my sins, some of which were major. I felt a unique spiritual power in the story of Jesus in the Gospels, and I decided I believed in his divinity, his sacrifice on the cross, and his resurrection from the dead. I resolved to be baptized into the Christian faith.

Around the same time as my initial acceptance of Jesus, I was developing a chronic illness that would become a disabling, life-altering condition. I found myself with severe chronic fatigue syndrome and neurological problems that made it increasingly difficult for me to work. At times, my health was so bad I thought I was dying—and despite several abnormal test results, doctors could not discover the root cause of my medical problems. Eventually I lost my job, was no longer able to have a social life, and ended up spending most of my time in bed, too sick to participate in society except through the internet.

Neither my baptism, nor my repeated prayers for healing, nor going down for an altar call in a conservative church I attended did anything to make me feel better. Rather than regaining the vigor of youth, I felt like a sick and tired 90-year-old man who was on his death bed, while still in my early 20's and not knowing why this was happening to me. I did not feel I had been born again, except that I believed in Jesus Christ. But where were the outward signs of my spiritual transformation? Modern evangelical Christianity would have us believe that if we are truly saved, good things will start happening in our life. Instead, my life was going to hell.

Was it possible that I never was *really* saved? Was it possible that I was still going to hell, not only on earth but also in the life hereafter, unless somehow I managed to convince God to fill me with the Holy Spirit I presumably had not yet received? Did God hate me? Why was it that so many people become Christians and begin an upward arc of improving health, wealth, success, and happiness—overcoming alcoholism, getting up out of a wheelchair or being cured of cancer, and all the other wonderful things they like to talk about in fundamentalist churches—yet for some strange reason, God was not doing things like this for me? I could only wonder whether it was possible that I was doomed to hell forever. If God wasn't saving me now, then how could I expect Him *ever* to save me? Perhaps the Calvinists were right, and I had been predestined from birth for damnation. The fires of my illness were only the first sign of the fires of hell that would one day consume my body and soul, tormenting me with an agony that would never end.

To add to my woes in the flesh, I began to suffer from troubles of the mind. A mild depression I had suffered periodically since adolescence escalated into major depressive disorder. The mild tendencies toward anxiety I had felt for years became a profound, gnawing unease within me that would never go away, punctuated by occasional panic

attacks that would leave me sapped of all emotional energy and begging on my knees for the Lord to intervene and change my life. My
prayers to God became increasingly plaintive, moaning lamentations,
filled with weeping and shaking, prostrations to the floor and pound-
ing fists of anger at the wrath that had been poured out upon me. Like
Job, I was filled with an acute sense of injustice—yet to make matters worse, I knew that I was a sinner, not a righteous man who was a
model of faithfulness. According to the Christian creed, I was deserv-
ing of divine punishment. But I didn't understand why my decision to
accept Jesus was not enough to spare me from further wrath. Hadn't
God forgiven me of my sins through the sacrifice of Jesus Christ I had
accepted? Why wasn't God willing to work miracles in my life? Did
God even hear my prayers?

In the depths of despair, I began to fear that no matter what I did,
no matter how many times I went to church or how fervent and fre-
quent my prayers, God simply didn't care about me. I was already one
of the lost; my supposed salvation must have been bogus. Being born
again was for other people, who were more fortunate to be part of
God's glorious plan as victorious Christians who would enjoy blessings in this life and paradise in the next. But for me, there was only a
life of continued illness and misery to look forward to, ending in the
likelihood of spending eternity in hell. After all, if God didn't hear my
plea for a better life on earth, why would He grant my request to be
admitted into heaven?

As I read the verses in the Bible about hell, I began to be filled with
a terror unlike anything I had ever felt before. A place of darkness,
weeping, wailing and gnashing of teeth, worms that never die, a fire
that is never quenched, burning and burning with no rest for its in-
habitants day or night—for ever and ever and ever. Could this really be
part of God's plan? Could it be the part that was meant for people like
me? Oh, the horror of it all! And the anger. The burning anger, bub-
bling up into a volcanic rage, at the way God treats His children. Why
had I even bothered to convert to Christianity? Why did God lead me
to this religion if He wasn't going to fill me with the Holy Spirit and enable me to be saved? Just so that I could know ahead of time what was
awaiting me in hell, so that God could make me suffer the loss of hope
and the anguish and terror, before I even got there?

In my darkest hour, God led me to a deeper understanding of Him and His plan—a plan that does not include eternal damnation for any being, but unfailing love and hope for all souls. This book has been my attempt to share in an easy-to-understand way some of what I had to learn the hard way. The God I have come to know is not the God of fundamentalist Christianity, but the God of Jesus and the apostles, a God we can worship in joyful adoration, unburdened by our fears of unworthiness. The true Christian God is a God of whom it can truly be said, "In Him there is no darkness at all." (1 John 1:5). "For men are not cast off by the LORD forever. Though He brings grief, He will show compassion, so great is His unfailing love." (Lam. 3:31-32). As John said, "God is love." (1 John 4:8,16). And as Paul said, "Love is patient, love is kind. It does not envy, it does not boast, it is not proud. It is not rude, it is not self-seeking, it is not easily angered, it keeps no record of wrongs. Love does not delight in evil but rejoices with the truth. It always protects, always trusts, always hopes, always perseveres. *Love never fails.*" (1 Cor. 13:4-8).

It is my hope that all Christians—and indeed all people—may learn about the God of love I have discovered, the God of a more joyful Christianity than the bad-news gospel that passes for the Good News of Christ in the minds of many souls. So many Christians are laboring and languishing in fear, their heart strangely empty because they have never felt real joy when they contemplate their God and their faith. The fire of hell has burned into the core of their being, leaving them scarred and scared. Legalistic efforts to please God through our works, as though we must earn His love in order to avoid condemnation, are the result of this erroneous creed—a creed that is responsible for much needless suffering and conflict, which deprives us of true peace within ourselves and in society. And so many people have not found faith in Christ at all, because they have thought that the fundamentalist message was true to the Bible and that God really is a monster. They would rather believe God doesn't even exist, rather than accept a religion that offers only fear and shame.

After a few years of being too ill to work, God has blessed me with renewed health. In 2005, while I was still chronically ill, I asked God to let me bring His peace to others, even if my own life might remain a difficult life of suffering. I started an online ministry at Christian-

Universalism.com to share the hope-inspiring all-inclusive Gospel I had discovered. The love of God filled me with a new energy and passion for life, and my health slowly began to improve. In 2007—feeling much better both physically and mentally—I succeeded in bringing together spiritual leaders from several denominational backgrounds to found the Christian Universalist Association, the first significant organization in decades to unite churches, ministries, and individuals in the teaching of Christian Universalism.

Through this organization as well as my own personal ministry, I am bringing the Gospel of hope and glad tidings of joy to hundreds of new people every day, many of whom are struggling to understand how the God of Jesus Christ could possibly maintain a burning hell for eternity as they have been taught in church. I am so happy to be able to share with the world that *the church is wrong!*—because Jesus, the Apostles, and the Bible are right: God is in the process of saving all souls and making them new in the image of Christ, and there is no eternal hell where some people will be condemned to suffer forever. It is my privilege and joy to be blessed with the opportunity to teach this message to as many as are willing to listen; to be a bold voice proclaiming God's Good News for all people.

God promises to "draw all men to Myself." (John 12:32). Truly, He won't stop until He finishes the job. God drew me until I escaped the hell of my fears and entered into the heaven of understanding. I was saved from the darkness, the mental torment of fundamentalism. I pray that all who are trapped in the hell I was in will feel the power of the Spirit drawing them into the Light, and will be reunited with the God who created them in Perfect Love—and right now, in this life, will feel a peace that knows neither beginning nor end.

Numb and Lukewarm Christians, and an Impotent Church

Tragically, stories of the descent into religious despair such as what I experienced are not uncommon. I have often received emails through my website in which frightened, angry, and despairing Christians—often young converts or those who have been raised in fundamentalism—pour out their innermost thoughts and feelings and ask me to help them overcome their obsessive fear of going to hell or seeing their non-Christian loved ones condemned there. Some people even experience severe mental health problems, such as I did, because of the fear of a damning god. God only knows how many people throughout history never escaped the insanity in this life because they never had the opportunity to learn about the real God's wonderfully benevolent nature.

I believe there is a spiritual cauterization that occurs because of belief in eternal hell. When we reject the hope for all souls, replacing it with an expectation that only some can ever be saved and the rest shall burn, our own heart and soul are burned and blackened and the Holy Spirit can no longer flow through us as strongly as it might otherwise. To stop the bleeding of our faith and to quell our pain and our tears at the thought of billions of unsaved souls forever in torment, we allow ourselves to become spiritually numb, half-dead. We refuse to ever really get to know God, to grow close to Him in more than a superficial way. Indeed, we cannot. For unless and until we are willing to confront the thing we hate the most about Christianity—the specter of damnation—we can never overcome and move forward on our spiritual journey. We must be ready to wrestle with God, and with ourselves, about this all-important issue. We will not find the resolution until we go beyond the brush-off approach, the simple catch phrases and juvenile explanations that serve only to mollify our fears, our sadness and our anger, by covering them up for the moment, never fully to be quenched.

In this book, we have explored the issue in some depth and seen that there is strong evidence for universalism as a fully Biblical Christian teaching. Moreover, we have seen that the Gospel itself, as it was originally taught by the apostles and the early church, was based on this concept as its very foundation—the idea that God is saving all people through a corrective process of judgment, so that all souls can someday be patterned after Christ. It is a completely different view of what Christianity is all about, compared to much of the Christian tradition that has been handed down to us by the church. Salvation is not about being saved *from* some endless and meaningless hell that lurks after death; it is about being raised beyond our present state of imperfection *into* the glorious divine destiny that God has planned for every human being.

Many Christians are lukewarm about sharing the Gospel because they do not understand it. The gospel they were taught is not the true

Gospel. It has been infected with a satanic virus that renders it spiritually dead and impotent, except for purposes of frightening people into submission. Even that doesn't work as well as it used to, as more people nowadays are opting instead for an atheistic, non-spiritual belief system as a way to get away from religious fundamentalism. Many churches try to focus on the aspects of the Gospel that have remained largely untouched by the virus of hell-based theology—things such as family, charity, community service, and peacemaking—but they can never fully witness to the amazing grace of God while secretly or quietly believing that some souls perhaps are irredeemable, beyond the salvific power of God, both in this life and the life to come.

This must change. Mainstream Christians must stop being embarrassed to share their faith because of fear of offending people's innate sensibilities with the horrible doctrine of damnation. We must relearn the Gospel, excising the falsehoods we have been taught, and proclaim the truth with confidence, knowing that there is nothing in the faith of Christ we need be embarrassed about. Fundamentalists must stop being overzealous, intolerant, and filled with a desire to save souls from damnation by converting them to a church creed. It is time for the new wine of Christian Universalism—a vintage that has spent centuries aging, buried in the wine-cellar, while people got drunk on inferior dregs. The new wine of the Gospel of universal salvation only seems new because we are just now discovering it as if for the first time! Let the world taste of this choice wine of Christian antiquity that has been preserved by God for the present day; and let the world celebrate, in the joy of reclaimed knowledge, His divine plan for all people.

The Most Important Choice We Face Today

The world today needs a fresh dose of hope, not fear. I believe the ultimate hope is through Christ, but the world is not hearing the message as it should be delivered. God's new covenant is not a legalistic, if-then promise like the covenant of Moses, upon which Muhammad based the religion of Islam long after Christ sought to end the curse of religious law. The covenant of Jesus Christ is an unconditional promise like the one given to Abraham. And it has been given to all souls—saints and sinners, believers and unbelievers alike. This is the hidden message of the Gospel, which has largely been forgotten throughout history. Today we need to bring it out of the tomb and resurrect it, so that the world can rise from the spiritual death of legalistic, exclusivistic, arrogant fundamentalism and be reborn into a new relationship with the Divine—a parent-child relationship of mutual love and trust, rather than a servile relationship based upon fear, threats of punishment, and the capricious whims of a jealous and angry god.

It cannot be stressed enough that *we become like the God we worship.* Perhaps one of the major reasons for terrorism and hatred is that the god of fundamentalism inspires terror and hates sinners with a passion so fierce that the fire of his anger will never go out, not even after ages and ages of burning vengeance. Fundamentalism, both Christian and non-Christian, is on the rise today. It must be stopped, before its fires consume our world.

Abdullah Thabit is the author of *The 20ᵗʰ Terrorist*, a book published in Syria in early 2006. He recounts his upbringing in Saudi Arabia among religious extremists, who emphasized the destiny of all "infidels" to go to hell and the threat of hell for anyone who does not rigidly follow radical Islam. He says he could easily have become one of the terrorist attackers who, in the name of their religion, hijacked airplanes and flew them into the World Trade Center towers on September 11, 2001. Thabit says of the ultra-religious sect he studied with as a youth, "We were taught that our Islam was correct and everyone else, including our families, was going to hell, a hell that resembled a slaughterhouse. And I wanted to be one of the select few who made it into heaven."[19] His descriptions of how he was indoctrinated with these fundamentalist beliefs are lurid and disturbing:

> "In the book, Thabit says one of his mentors, Yahya, took him on weekly trips to the cemetery, after midnight, where they would lie for hours in freshly dug graves and listen in the dark to a sermon about hell played on the car cassette player. The cleric would describe a hell filled with snakes, leaping fire and sinners stripped naked hanging on hooks, their skins peeled off. Life is temporary and the hereafter is forever, the cleric warned. Thabit often wept from fear. 'When we

[19] Ambah, Faiza Saleh. "The Would-Be Terrorist's Explosive Tell-All Tale." *The Washington Post*, July 24, 2006, p. C4.

left from there, I wanted Yahya to tell me anything I could do to be saved from hellfire and from that terror,' he writes. ...

"When Thabit turned 17, the group suggested he go to Afghanistan for jihad, or holy war, training. But he was afraid and said he didn't feel quite ready yet. ...

"'I feel very sad,' Thabit said. 'I wish they [the extremists] could live a life full of love and art and music. I wish they could regain their humanity. But their lives have been stolen from them and they don't even know it.'"[20]

It is not only Muslims who are having their lives stolen away by religious fundamentalism; it is also many Christians. Nobody is immune to these dangers, if they believe that most people are consigned for eternity to a cosmic torture chamber because of God's unquenchable anger and hatred of non-believers. Similar beliefs about the nature of God and His plan for human beings lead ultimately to similar consequences in people's lives and our world. If it's not suicide bombers and acts of terrorism, it may be ordinary suicide by sensitive young people and aggressive wars by our leaders in the old spirit of the Crusades. Some fundamentalist Christians are so eager for the "Rapture"—when their god will supposedly whisk true believers out of this world leaving everyone else to burn in a fiery apocalypse that is the prelude to the eternal fires of hell—that they are eager to see calamity and destruction in the earth, believing this to be a sign of God's impending judgment upon the wicked.

The most important choice the world faces today is whether to follow the religion of Fundamentalism—by whatever name it goes, in any of its forms—or the Christian Gospel of Universalism. We must choose, and quickly! We cannot afford to sit idly by, watching our planet being taken over by the scourge of fundamentalist anger and fruitless conflict. In an age of nuclear bombs and other weapons of mass destruction, the stakes are too high. This world cannot endure another century reaping the fruits of religious fundamentalism without seeing the field thoroughly burned up in the process.

---

[20] Ibid.

Make no mistake about it, the only way to put out the raging fire of hatred in our world is to put out the fire of hell in people's hearts. I have shown in this book that the concept of hell and God's judgment has been completely misunderstood by believers in traditional religion. Consequently, the joy has been sucked out of Christianity, and hope has been lost for a multitude of souls—perhaps never to regain it in this lifetime. As truth-seeking Christians or open-minded spiritual seekers, we have a responsibility to question our assumptions about the Bible, about religion, and above all about God and His plan. There is yet hope for our souls and our world, even when we doubt it is possible.

The fact is, the exclusive salvation and eternal damnation of fundamentalism is nothing more than a lie—a powerful lie with a long history, but a lie that must finally be defeated by the truth. The Bible teaches that hell is temporary, purgatorial, and reformative rather than everlasting, tormenting, and vindictive. The Bible teaches that all people are God's beloved children, and that He is raising us up through trials and tests and experiences of growth until we are ready for greater things. The Bible teaches that God has an unfailing plan to save *all* people by correcting us according to the example of Christ, and even more, transforming us into his perfect image, so that we can fully express the divine light that is within *all* of us—so that we can make this earth a world filled with the Light that "shines in the darkness, and the darkness did not overcome it." (John 1:5 NRSV).

That, my friends, is the Good News of Christian Universalism. That is the original Gospel of Jesus Christ. The Light of God shall never go out—not on this planet, not in this universe, and not in the innermost essence of any being. We only must discover it and embrace it. And when we do, our hearts will overflow with joy and our Christianity will make perfect sense for the first time, in a way we will want to shout from the rooftops. In a way that can truly change our lives and let the long-awaited Kingdom of Heaven dawn upon the earth. *Amen (let it be so).*

An Invitation

If you agree with the Gospel of Jesus Christ presented in this book—whether you have never before professed faith in Christ, or you are a Christian who has come to see your faith in a new way—I invite you to join me in praying this prayer:

O God, Heavenly Father,

Thank You for showing me that You are a God of love for all people, that I am Your divine offspring, and that You have planned and purposed before the foundation of the world for me and all my brothers and sisters in Your human family to be brought up into the station of Christ, our Lord and Elder Brother who was sent to earth to show us the way.

Father, I pray that You will guide me and assist me in my walk with Christ, as I strive to grow each day from this day forward, to become more like Christ and to manifest Your Light in my life. Let me live in Christ, of Christ, through Christ, for Christ, in all things at all times. I dedicate myself to the path of Christ today and always.

When I stumble, Lord, offer me Your helping hand. When I feel like I can't go on, strengthen me with the power of Your Holy Spirit. When I make a mistake, Father, forgive me and do not let me dwell upon my sin, but encourage me to learn from what I have done wrong or failed to do right, to improve my soul so that I will do better next time. If I need discipline, let me receive it. If I need tenderness and compassion, let me have it.

Above all, I ask You, my Lord and my God, to help me share Your love with others. Let me be a beacon of light and truth in this world, so that all those I meet may learn of Your amazing and unconditional love for them, even as You loved Your firstborn son, Jesus Christ. Let it be known to all people that Your love is not as a man loves a creature or a thing, which he may later hate and cast aside, but it is the love of a parent for a child—a love that can never fail.

Let them know that even when they suffer, they do not suffer in vain. For it was not out of hatred that You allowed Your beloved Son to be nailed to the cross, but out of love for us, who have already received the blessing of his sacrifice. For he showed us—You showed us—that no matter how much it may appear that You have abandoned a man to torment, no one is ever forsaken. Let my eyes be opened, along with the eyes of all creation, to the power of the resurrection as the remedy for the cross of suffering upon which all beings groan in anticipation of the restoration of all things. For I believe that if You can raise Jesus from the dead and glorify him, truly You are a God for which no good thing is impossible.

Heavenly Father, I ask that You will bless all people today with the knowledge of Your love and Your unfailing plan of salvation. In this age, let the world unite in brotherhood and reconciliation. Let us put aside our differences of religion, of nationality, of the color of the skin, of whatever else that may divide us; and let us see one another for who we really are: the children of the same Almighty God, all of whom will be raised up and none of whom will be left behind. Fill our hearts, Lord,

with the promise of hope for all people. Let us all experience the joy that comes from hearing Your Good
News. And let me do all that I can to share it, and to
help make Your wonderful plan a reality.

I pray all of these things in Jesus' name. Amen.

The next step is to join together with other Christians who believe
as we do, for fellowship, worship, evangelism, and service to people in
need. I encourage you to seek out a community of faith founded on
the teaching of Christian Universalism. Please visit the website of the
Christian Universalist Association, www.christianuniversalist.org, for a
list of churches and home meeting groups with ministers or leaders who
believe in the ultimate salvation of all. If you cannot find a church or
group in your area that is right for you, the CUA would be happy to help
you start one. You can contact me by email through the CUA website
or through my personal ministry site, Christian-Universalism.com, and
we can talk about ideas and resources for church planting and spreading
the Gospel.

Divine blessings,
Eric Stetson

CPSIA information can be obtained at www.ICGtesting.com
Printed in the USA
BVOW07s0136151214

379402BV00001B/184/P